EXPLORING WATER WITH YOUNG CHILDREN

OTHER BOOKS IN THE YOUNG SCIENTIST SERIES:

exploring water with young children

Ingrid Chalufour and Karen Worth
Education Development Center, Inc.

The *Young Scientist* Series

Redleaf Press
St. Paul, Minnesota
www.redleafpress.org

Published by Redleaf Press
a division of Resources for Child Caring
10 Yorkton Court
St. Paul, MN 55117
Visit us online at www.redleafpress.org.

Written by Ingrid Chalufour and Karen Worth with Robin Moriarty, Jeff Winokur, and Sharon Grollman.

Redleaf Press books are available at a special discount when purchased in bulk for special premiums and sales promotions. For details, contact the sales manager at 800-423-8309.

This book was written with the support of National Science Foundation Grant ESI-9818737. However, any opinions, findings, conclusions, and/or recommendations herein are those of the authors and do not necessarily reflect the views of NSF.

Library of Congress Cataloging-in-Publication Data

Chalufour, Ingrid.
    Exploring water with young children / Ingrid Chalufour and Karen Worth.
    p. cm.—(The young scientist series)
    Includes index.
    ISBN-10: 1-929610-54-8 (pbk.)
    ISBN-13: 978-1-929610-54-9
    1. Water—Study and teaching (Early childhood) 2. Water—Experiments. I. Worth, Karen. II. Title.

GB658.C43 2005
372.35'044—dc22
                                                                    2004029765

Manufactured in the United States of America

12 11 10 09 08 07 06 05   1 2 3 4 5 6 7 8

The Young Scientist Series was developed by a team of early childhood educators at Education Development Center, Inc., which was funded by a grant from the National Science Foundation and led by Ingrid Chalufour and Karen Worth. Listed below are the members of the team, all of whom contributed substantially to the work from its conceptualization to the final product.

INGRID CHALUFOUR has designed and conducted professional development programs for staff in child care programs, Head Start, public schools, and social service agencies for more than thirty-five years.

SHARON GROLLMAN, a senior research associate at EDC's Center for Children and Families, has developed educational materials for more than twenty years. Prior to coming to EDC, she was part of a research team in early childhood education.

ROBIN MORIARTY taught young children in the Boston area for fourteen years before she joined EDC. Currently, her work includes curriculum development, leading professional development programs, and working with early childhood centers.

JEFFREY WINOKUR has worked in early childhood and science education for over twenty years as an instructor in education at Wheelock College and a senior research associate at EDC. He also conducts workshops and training for communities in science for young children.

KAREN WORTH has been a senior scientist at EDC for the past thirty-five years. She is also a graduate-level instructor at Wheelock College in the early childhood education department. Her work includes the development of science curriculum and professional development programs, as well as consultation in science education for young children.

contents

acknowledgments

The Young Scientist Series was developed by the project staff of the Tool Kit for Early Childhood Science Education housed at Education Development Center, Inc. (EDC), with funding from the National Science Foundation.

Numerous educators and consultants contributed to the development and field testing of the series. We would like to thank the following people for their contributions to this work.

DEVELOPMENT TEACHERS

Cindy Hoisington
Lucia McAlpin
Carole Moyer
Rebecca Palacios
Susan Steinsick

PILOT TEACHERS

Colette Auguste
Liana Bond
Imelda DeCosta
Marlene Dure
Frank Greene
Karen Hoppe
Terry Kuchenmeister
Stuart Lui
Maureen McIntee
Susan Miller
Katherine O'Leary
Carolyn Robinson
Ellen Sulek
Laurie Wormstead
Tiffany Young

FIELD TEST SITES

Bainbridge Island Child Care
  Centers, Bainbridge Island, WA
Barre Town School, Barre, VT
Berlin Elementary School,
  Berlin, VT
Blackwater Community School,
  Coolidge, AZ
Blue Hill Avenue Early Education
  Center, Boston, MA

Bright Horizons at Preston
  Corners, Cary, NC
Childspace Day Care Centers,
  Philadelphia, PA
City of Phoenix Head Start,
  Phoenix, AZ
Cisco Family Connection Bright
  Horizons, Milpitas, CA
East Montpelier Elementary
  School, East Montpelier, VT
Epic Head Start, Yakima, WA
Fort Worth Museum of Science
  and History, Fort Worth, TX
Four Corners School, East
  Montpelier, VT
K–5 Inquiry-Based Science
  Program, Seattle Public
  Schools, WA
Louisiana Tech University Early
  Childhood Education Center,
  Ruston, LA
Motorola Childcare and Education
  Center, Schaumburg, IL
Pasadena Unified School District,
  Pasadena, CA
Phoenix Head Start, Phoenix, AZ
Portage Private Industry Council
  Head Start, Ravenna, OH
School for Early Learning, Spring
  Branch Independent School
  District, Houston, TX
Thomson Early Childhood Center,
  Seattle, WA
UMC Child Development Lab,
  Columbia, MO

Valle Imperial Project in Science,
  El Centro, CA
William H. Rowe School,
  Yarmouth, ME
Young Achievers Science and
  Mathematics Pilot School,
  Boston, MA

ADVISORY BOARD MEMBERS

Douglas Clements
David Dickinson
George Forman
Linda French
Marilou Hyson
Stephanie Johnson
Diane Levin
Mary Jane Moran
Carolyn Vieria
Sandra Williams
Diane Willow

CONSULTANTS

Mary Eisenberg
Pat Fitzsimmons
Ben Mardell
Janet Sebell

We also would like to acknowledge
the following people at EDC:

Erica Fields, Research Assistant
Kerry Ouellet, Editor and
  Production Manager
Susan Weinberg, Senior
  Administrative Assistant

introduction

"In a world filled with the products of scientific inquiry, scientific literacy has become a necessity for everyone. Everyone needs to use scientific information to make choices that arise every day. Everyone needs to be able to engage intelligently in public discourse and debate about important issues that involve science and technology. And everyone deserves to share in the excitement and personal fulfillment that can come from understanding and learning about the natural world" (National Research Council 1996, 1).

"If a child is to keep alive his inborn sense of wonder, he needs the companionship of at least one adult who can share it, rediscovering with him the joy, the excitement, and the mystery of the world" (Carson 1965).

How do we keep alive this inborn sense of wonder in early childhood classrooms? How can teachers provide children with appropriate experiences and guidance? Using the Young Scientist series is one way. But before we describe the series and how to use this guide, we would like to share a few responses to two important questions: (1) Why is science knowledge important? and (2) Why should we start in the preschool years?

Why Is Science Knowledge Important?

One goal of science is to understand the natural world. Knowing some science can help us explain why things happen, such as why water evaporates and why plants grow in particular locations, what causes disease, and how electricity works. Scientific knowledge also can help us predict what might happen—when a hurricane may hit the coast or how severe the flu will be this winter.

But science is more than knowledge; it is also a process of exploration that we call *scientific inquiry*. When scientists try to learn something about events,

objects, or materials, they observe, wonder, and ask questions. And they go further and focus on one question, predicting what they think they might find out and setting up an investigation. They observe closely, using their senses and tools to collect and record data and evidence. Through analysis of their data and reflection on all they've done, they develop new ideas and theories and communicate those to others.

Most of us are not scientists, but in many small ways, we do science. When you ask the question, "How much light does my geranium need to flower well?" then test the different possibilities by putting one in the sun and one in the shade to find your answer, you are doing science. When you compare two pens, predict which one you think will work best for the drawing you are making, and then try them out, you are doing science. When you use a book to find out what kind of birdseed will attract cardinals, you are doing science.

Whether we work in a lab or a school, chart the courses of hurricanes, or want to learn about sound, we all have questions—scientists and nonscientists, adults and children alike—and we all use some of the basic tools of scientific inquiry. Given the opportunity to explore and discover, we can feel the sense of wonder, joy, and excitement that Rachel Carson describes above.

Why Should We Start Science in the Preschool Years?

Children's curiosity about the natural world, their "inborn sense of wonder," is a powerful catalyst for their work and play. With this curiosity and the need to make sense of the world, children are motivated to ask questions, explore how things work, and look closely at the natural world around them.

But in today's world, children's experiences and their opportunities to do science are often limited—confined too frequently to the passive and secondhand experience of the television or video game. Modern technology also has hidden from view some of the basic ways in which things work. Our food comes from stores and few children have seen or engaged in growing and processing it. Toys that were once pushed or pulled or rolled now have hidden motors and batteries to drive them and a switch to turn them on and off.

Science curriculum is important in the early childhood classroom so that "doing science" becomes a natural and critical part of children's early learning. With carefully selected materials and thoughtful guidance, children's explorations will encourage them to observe more closely, develop new ideas about the world, and build a foundation of experiences and ideas on which to construct later understanding. Science in early childhood classrooms also provides a rich context in which children can develop other important skills, including large- and small-muscle control, language and early mathematical understanding, and cooperation.

What Is the Young Scientist Series?

The Young Scientist series is a science curriculum for children who are three to five years old. Each of the teacher guides provides background information and detailed guidance on how to incorporate science into your daily program using many of the materials you already have in the classroom in new ways. *Discovering Nature with Young Children* is about the living things right outside the classroom door. *Exploring Water with Young Children* takes a new look at the water table, and *Building Structures with Young Children* challenges children to use building materials found in the classroom to explore questions of how to make things strong,

tall, or elegant. Each study can take several months or extend over longer periods of time.

The Young Scientist series is not about learning and repeating facts, information, and vocabulary with little direct experience. It is not following a set of directed activities or learning the scientific method. It is not a week focused on bears and it is not observing random objects on a science table. The Young Scientist series makes science the work and play of exploring materials and phenomena, while providing opportunities for children to learn from that experience. Young children may do this as they engage in fantasy and dramatic play—creating magic potions at the water table or building a home for the make-believe turtle in the block area, or examining the worms they discovered digging in the sand area. They may do science as they challenge themselves or invent a game: "Who can build the highest tower or empty the water bucket the fastest?" They also may engage in exploration as young scientists, wondering and questioning and seeking to make sense of the world: "What would happen if I rolled the ball from the very top of the ramp? What does my worm need to live? I wonder if I can find an anthill near the one we found yesterday."

As they explore and interact with one another, young children try to make sense of what they see and do. They develop early theories about why things are the way they are, act the way they do, and how they relate to one another. As their experience broadens and their thinking deepens, their ideas and theories become more plausible and closer to current understandings in science.

Exciting science experiences for young children do not just happen. The Young Scientist series establishes your important role to ensure that children's play and ideas about science are focused, deepened, and challenged. The following examples illustrate the differences between activity-based water study, a thematic approach, and an in-depth exploration of the science of water.

Teacher A notices that several of her children seem to enjoy the water table at choice time each day. Wishing to extend children's experiences with water, she plans for the following week to have a number of days of water activities that are different from their experiences at the water table, and in which the whole class can participate. On Monday she provides small groups with three different colors of water—red, yellow, and blue—eyedroppers, and empty cups or egg cartons in which children can mix the colors and create new ones. On Tuesday she provides white coffee filters for children to find out what happens when drops of the colored water are put onto the coffee filters. On Wednesday she puts ice cubes or snow into the water table. She encourages children to see what happens to the ice or snow as they use the droppers to put the colored water on it. Thursday is planned as a day to see what happens when children mix powders, such as instant pudding or baking powder, with small amounts of water. And on Friday, as a culmination of the week, she takes the children outside to make bubbles with a variety of materials.

In this example, the teacher planned to provide children with a variety of experiences that relate to water's various properties. The children are presented with a wide array of materials and are actively engaged in a variety of exciting hands-on experiences with water. But while water is at the center of each of the activities, it isn't clear which science concepts are the focus, and what role the teacher plays in helping children think about these concepts. Although the children use water to mix colors and to drip colored water through filters, these experiences are more about color than they are about water. Wednesday's activity involves observing water as it changes from a solid, such as ice or snow, to a liquid. It is an appropriate water science activity but there is no further exploration, such as freezing water or melting ice cubes in different locations. Thursday's and Friday's activities are related to different properties of water, but again these brief unrelated experiences will not support children's deeper understanding of properties of water.

Teacher B also finds some of her children excited by their experiences at the water table. She gathers many materials: several bottles with colorful liquids for the science center, such as a tornado tube or an oil and water "wave" bottle; a fish bowl with some goldfish, also for the science center; books about water, rain, clouds, and bodies of water for the class library; watercolor paints for the art area; materials such as cotton balls to make cloud collages, also for the art area; and large charts with songs and chants about water (such as "Itsy Bitsy Spider") for the classroom walls. She has added some blue construction paper to the block area to represent a river, lake, or moat that can be incorporated into children's block play. She has added measuring spoons and cups to the math center to introduce liquid measurements. Teacher B introduces the project with a class discussion asking children to share their experiences with water. She identifies the

areas in the classroom where there are water-related activities and encourages children to spend time at each over the course of the next week or two. During this time she moves through the classroom supporting children's play, and during group time she encourages children to talk about their water experiences. Toward the end of the project, the children make a special trip to a local outdoor fountain to experience water in a different setting.

In this example, children are surrounded by water activities. The block area, the library, the art area, and the math center have water-related activities, all of which address basic literacy, math, and social skills. The children are very engaged, and the visit to the fountain turns out to be a wonderful trip. But this project with its water theme has little to do with scientific inquiry and in-depth exploration of appropriate science concepts over time.

Teacher C also responds to her children's interest in the water table. But she decides that this interest could be the beginning of a long-term exploration of the observable properties of water. She identifies several concepts children can grapple with. Over the course of two weeks, in addition to the various containers the children have for pouring and filling, she introduces new materials to the water table, carefully chosen to focus on some of these properties, such as funnels and clear plastic tubing to explore water's downward flow, and turkey basters that can make air bubbles and help move the water in other directions. She collects some books that focus on the physical properties of water and contain up-close photographs or drawings of water. She takes photos of children as they explore at the water table, and encourages children to talk about their experiences at the next day's group meeting, using the photographs to help children remember what they had done. As children continue to explore water and talk about their experiences, she helps them construct more complex water systems at the water table. She opens an additional water center in the room, allowing more children to explore how water flows in smaller streams. She provides eyedroppers so children can begin to notice that drops of water actually have a shape. On a rainy day, she takes the class outside to see where they find water, how it moves down roofs and down spouts, and where it pools and where it gets absorbed into the ground. By doing this she encourages children to connect what they are observing outdoors with their indoor experiences. Throughout the exploration, Teacher C encourages children to talk about what they notice and wonder about, and to draw and photograph their water experiences.

As in the other examples, children in this classroom enjoyed playing with water, but in this case they are also engaged in active, hands-on science inquiry that illustrates the approach of the Young Scientist series. The teacher builds on the children's interests and has defined a clear set of science concepts to guide their work with water. She encourages them to conduct their own observations and explorations. While many other skills are practiced and learned, science is in the foreground. Using the outdoor experiences, as well as indoor experiences and books, she promotes creative, deep exploration and children's use of inquiry.

The teacher focuses the children's attention on important physical properties of water:

- Water flows down, unless acted upon

- Water takes the shape of its container

- Water sticks to itself (cohesion)

- Water sticks to other materials (adhesion)

- Air makes bubbles in water and rises to the surface

She encourages deeper thinking to enrich their experiences without interfering in their own process of questioning and exploration. As she does this the children develop their skills in the following areas:

- Observing closely

- Describing what they see

- Raising questions

- Investigating

- Representing things and ideas

- Discussing

As you continue to read and begin to implement, you will learn more about science for young children and what they can do. You will also learn about how to make it possible for children to engage in the rich science exploration exemplified by Teacher C. As you teach, keep in mind these basic principles in the Young Scientist series.

- All three- to five-year-olds can successfully experience rich, in-depth scientific inquiry.

- The content of the science learning draws from children's experiences, is interesting and engaging, and can be explored directly and deeply over time. Expectations are developmentally appropriate; that is, they are realistic and tailored to the strengths, interests, and needs of individual children.

- Discussion, expression, representation, and reflection are critical ways in which children make meaning and develop theories from their active work. Children learn from one another.

- Teachers can take on specific roles and use particular strategies to actively support and guide children's science learning.

Rationale and Goals

Water is everywhere. It is in oceans and lakes. It flows in rivers and streams, as well as through the pipes of our houses and schools. It falls from the sky in the form of rain, snow, or hail. And, of course, it is essential for life.

All children have had experiences with water. They bathe in it, drink it, and get wet when it rains. And, when given the opportunity, most children love to play with it! Many early childhood settings support this play by providing water tables or by taking some time to observe what happens to water during rain showers.

The experiences described in this book will take children further by focusing their explorations and providing opportunities to deepen their understanding of liquids and the properties of water. Questions such as, "Can you find ways to stop the water from coming out of the tube? What happens when you put more water into the container? What happens to drops of water when you tilt the plate?" focus children's attention. Through their explorations, you can help children notice, question, and think about some of the properties of water. At the same time, you will help them develop science skills as they learn to collect and analyze data, represent their ideas, and share them with others. Such experiences will help children to build a foundation on which to develop a later understanding of the states of matter.

The specific goals of the exploration are to provide opportunities for children to

- Develop basic science process skills.

- Develop ideas about some of water's basic properties such as that water flows, takes the shape of its container, sticks to itself, and sticks more or less strongly to other materials; and that objects can sink or float in water. There is also a brief focus on air and how air bubbles in water always rise to the surface.

- Develop scientific dispositions, including eagerness to learn, curiosity, and interest in exploring water with a variety of materials.

The Classroom Environment

One of the most important roles you play in this exploration is creating an environment and culture in your classroom that supports and encourages children's exploration of water. The classroom must convey the excitement, challenge, and wonder of exploring water with a variety of materials. Some of the characteristics of such an environment and culture follow.

The Importance of Water Exploration

A supportive environment will convey the importance of exploring water. By providing a wide range of materials for water play, such as tubing, connectors, basters that squirt, containers with holes, and pumps, you create an environment in which children are challenged to explore water in a number of ways. A supportive environment provides enough time, space, and access to water so children can try out numerous and varied ideas. Posters or photographs of water (such as of fountains, rivers, or waterfalls) placed around the classroom on the walls and books highlighting the properties of water provide children with a sense for the many ways water is part of our lives and environment.

An Emphasis on Inquiry

When children explore water, they ask questions and think about what their observations tell them. How can I move water through tubes? Will this piece of wood sink if I push it under the water? How will a funnel help to get water into the tube? How will the Y-connector change the water flow? Can I invent a machine to make lemonade? An environment that supports water exploration encourages such questions and ideas, and the investigations that follow. It emphasizes the importance of gathering data by having appropriate tools on hand and time to explore. This environment is full of children's ongoing dialogue and work as well as photographs, charts, and panels communicating the value of documentation and recording.

Sharing Observations and Ideas

In an environment supportive of water exploration, children are encouraged to share observations and ideas through small and large group discussions, and they learn to listen to what others have to say. They share their records of what they have done and their ideas about science concepts, such as how water can be made to move up, why some things float, and why water drops look different on different materials. They learn that ideas are valued and important whether right or wrong; that people may have different ideas; and that one can learn by asking questions of others. They also learn that they need to share how and why they know what they know as well as what they know.

Documentation and Recording

Scientists spend a great deal of time documenting what they see and think—using careful sketches, photographs, and descriptive words to most accurately remember their experiences. They use their notes to reflect with others and find patterns in their observations. Children can begin to develop these skills no matter their level of development. In an environment that supports water exploration, materials for representation are easily available and children's work is used to discuss their ideas and to stimulate more focused investigations.

Children as Water Explorers

This exploration is designed to provide experiences over time in which children can engage in multiple ways, depending on who they are and what they bring. You may find that some children are immediately drawn into the exploration, using everything you set out. Other children may be more reluctant, shying away from water. Some children may become engaged quickly, but then leave the water table after only a short time. How children approach this exploration, and what they learn, is influenced by a range of factors including the different experiences, needs, skills, and ideas that young children bring. As you prepare for this exploration, you will need to consider these factors.

PRIOR EXPERIENCES

Young children bring to water exploration their own ideas, interests, and beliefs based in experience and culture, and tempered by their developmental level. Depending on the environment in which they have lived, some children may have had many opportunities to explore and play with water both indoors and out; others may have had few. You might find some children will spend a great deal of time being soothed by the sensation of water; however, a few children may have difficulty with the sensation of water and may need to be introduced to it gradually in small quantities.

DIVERSE STRENGTHS AND CHALLENGES

Any class presents you with a diverse group of children. The Young Scientist series presents an ideal curriculum for diverse classrooms. All children can explore materials and objects; all children try to make sense of their environment. Each child in your classroom can engage with science and contribute to the classroom learning whether she is three or five years old, speaks English or Spanish or Creole at home, is typically developing or has a special need.

Exploring water relies heavily on children's firsthand experiences with water. Be sure that all children, including those with disabilities, have opportunities to explore water. As you plan, consider environmental adaptations you may need to make (such as how to arrange the space, how to place the materials so that all children know where to find them and can access them easily). Also think about curriculum adaptations (such as using visual cues or body language to convey information to children whose first language is not English) and materials adaptations (such as having buckets of water on a table or outside if a child cannot easily reach into the water table) that can support children's participation. Remember, some children may have little experience engaging in play, either alone or with others, and may need you to model and encourage.

COMMUNICATION SKILLS

As with all science, describing and recording what is planned, what is done, what is observed, and what happens is essential. Children will have varying levels of observation, language, and representational skills depending on their experience and developmental level. Some children may not have the use of many words to describe what they have done and may prefer to use their bodies and actions instead. Others may draw, but water, especially moving water, is very difficult to draw for even the most adept children. Although some will have difficulty drawing water, they may be able to draw the tubes and other materials in the water systems they create. In other instances, you may want to draw the materials and encourage children to draw or show you where the water traveled through the system. Still other children will document what they see using additional forms of representation, including three-dimensional materials and their bodies. It is important to encourage thinking and representation without expecting or pushing children to go beyond their capabilities. A camera for documenting children's experiences is strongly recommended for *Exploring Water with Young Children*.

CHILDREN'S IDEAS

Because all young children have had some experiences with water, they all have ideas and theories about it, which may be more or less accurate. *Exploring Water with Young Children* will give children many experiences with which to modify their ideas and theories and build new ones. But do not expect children to "correct" their initial ideas based on this exposure alone, and do not try to correct them directly. Through conversation, questions, and gentle probing, some children will come to new understandings, more reasonable, but not necessarily more accurate, than their old ones. Other children will need repeated exposure to ideas and experiences over extended periods of time to let go of old ideas and begin to refine and deepen their understanding.

The questions children have also may be very different from the ones you have. You cannot know what every child in your group is thinking, but you may get an idea of different children's points of view by listening to, questioning, and observing children as they explore. It also is helpful to think about some of the typical ideas and questions young children have about some of the basic science concepts related to exploring water.

Science Exploration through Play

Play is fundamental to children's development, and they approach much of what they do through play. Children engage in many kinds of play when exploring water, including dramatic or symbolic play, exploratory play, and constructive play (Eisenberg 2000). Symbolic play occurs throughout *Exploring Water with Young Children* as children cook, make potions, set up lemonade factories, and go on boat rides.

Regardless of children's fantasy contexts, these situations offer opportunities to extend their thinking about the science of water through encouragement and questions, such as "Can you add two more drops to your potion?", "How will you be able to get the lemonade into the bottle?", and "Will your boat be able to take more passengers?" Some children will find the process of exploring water with a variety of materials intriguing in itself, and will engage in exploratory play as they try to find easier ways to get water through tubes or examine a pump at work. Other children will spend time in constructive play as they create water systems of tubes attached to each other to move water in a variety of ways.

Connections between Science Outcomes and Other Domains

As you provide opportunities for your children to explore water, and guide them in their development of science inquiry skills, you will see growth in language, literacy, mathematics, and social skills, as well as in children's approaches to learning. The charts that appear in the appendix (pp. 120–121) shows the connections between science inquiry outcomes as we define them in the Young Scientist series and the outcomes of other subject areas taken from the Head Start Child Outcomes Framework.

Mathematics is one of the languages scientists use to record and reflect on their observations and to communicate their ideas to others. Exploring water with a variety of materials provides children with many opportunities to develop and use their mathematical ideas. Children will be exposed to basic measurement as they pour from one container to another,

comparing volume and capacity. They will be encouraged to develop mathematical language as they describe location (in/out, up/down) and movement (fast/slow) of water, comparison (more/less) of volume, and shape (round/flat) of water and the containers. Some children will simply experience these mathematical concepts, others will talk about them, and still others may use them explicitly as they explore water. Scientists also communicate with words. As children communicate their findings, participate in discussions, and represent their experiences they are certainly increasing their language and literacy skills. In fact, research suggests that engaging children in rich science experiences provides a context and a purpose for meaningful language and literacy learning. By engaging with science, children build their vocabulary while developing an ability to communicate their ideas.

Such a capacity for oral language provides the foundation for all literacy learning. Children also learn about the importance of books as they use them to get ideas about what water looks like in rivers, streams, and drops. They learn to record their observations, explanations, and ideas about properties of water by using multiple forms of representation, including drawings, simple graphs, and writing. Such representations provide a visible record that encourages children to reflect on and talk about their theories and what they have discovered.

Science is a social activity. Whether in person or through other means of communication, scientists exchange ideas, build on one another's work, and often collaborate on science investigations. As children pursue their questions about water's properties, they need to work together to compare findings. Together their individual ideas can suggest a bigger picture and new ideas—sharing and connecting tubes can create larger water systems. Such collaborative work (that involves sharing materials and ideas) provides children with significant opportunities for developing their social skills.

Making the Most of the Curriculum

Teachers who implement the Young Scientist series will use a specific approach to teaching: a set of strategies that balance the children's rich explorations with some more structured activities. This curriculum and the many accompanying tools and resources are designed to support you as you learn to use this approach. As you prepare to implement *Exploring Water with Young Children*, we encourage you to focus on four basic aspects of teaching that may be new to you: the science, the physical environment of the classroom, time and scheduling, and the facilitation and guidance of children's learning.

SCIENCE

You do not need to be a scientist to implement this curriculum. But in order to be responsive to children's explorations, you need to recognize and experience the science phenomena children are experiencing. There is no better way to build this understanding than to engage with the science. When you observe a child working to connect two pieces of tubing, you will be much better at guiding her if you have had experiences doing this on your own. When children raise questions about how to make water move up or sideways, your observations and experiences will help you suggest what children might focus on and what you might show them in a book or tell them. You will appreciate the challenge of drawing a water system if you have tried it yourself. Before introducing *Exploring Water with Young Children* to children, take time to explore water yourself. You will find activities to guide you in step 1 of the "Getting Ready" section on p. 13.

PHYSICAL ENVIRONMENT

Science for young children is about investigating real things, developing new ideas and theories, and sharing them with others. The richer and more varied the environment is, the richer and more varied the experiences the children will have. In addition, children's exploration will be more independent and sustained if the tools they need are readily available where and when they need them. You will find guidelines for setting up this environment in steps 3 and 4 of the "Getting Ready" section and in the preparation section of each step. Additional ideas are provided in the "Resources" section.

TIME AND SCHEDULING

Scientific inquiry takes time. Finding out how water flows through or is affected by different materials can take weeks of choice time. Focused inquiries into water flow in large and small streams, sinking and floating, and drops can last for weeks even when children focus on more than one aspect of water at a time. A typical schedule often does not include regular time periods of forty-five minutes to an hour and yet this is what is needed for groups of children to have the opportunity to study something closely. Often the program calls for a new theme or topic weekly or every two weeks, but *Exploring Water with Young Children* should go on at least a couple of months. In fact, as all your children become engaged, you may find the water exploration going on for three or more months.

FACILITATING AND GUIDING LEARNING

With your own water exploration under your belt, a physical environment that invites and supports children's inquiry, and a schedule that allows the time, the stage is set for the most important part of teaching—your interactions with the children. For some, there may be some new strategies to learn, new expectations required, and old approaches to let go of. This guide is designed to help you become a teacher of science for your children—engaging them in science and focusing and deepening their experiences and thinking. The step-by-step guide is designed to help you as you learn new roles and approaches.

Involve Families

Families are important to *Exploring Water with Young Children*. In cases where parents are not the sole caregivers, you can involve a grandparent, foster parent, aunt, uncle, older sibling, or cousin. As you involve families, consider how culture might influence a child's water play. For example, some families may discourage water play at home; some may have come from places where water is scarce or abundant; and others may not want children to get wet, particularly when the weather is cold outside. Talk with family members to learn about their cultures and children's experiences. This knowledge will help you engage families appropriately and respectfully.

And families have much to share about their children. Individual children may have had interesting and/or problematic experiences with water that are important to know. Some children may spend time playing with water at home, or may have a small stream nearby. Others may have had a bad experience being criticized for wanting to play with water, or are frightened of water. Families can provide you with important clues about such experiences as well as what materials intrigue their children, what questions they have, and what strategies you might use to support children's learning.

Take steps at the beginning to inform families about *Exploring Water with Young Children*—what you will be doing, what children will learn, and why this is important for children's development. Feel free to use or adapt the sample letter on p. 106 that introduces families to the exploration. If a caregiver does not speak English, find someone to help you translate the letter or make an audiotape in their home language. Also invite families into the classroom or host a family night where families can experience firsthand the importance of your science explorations and experiment with ways to promote children's water explorations at home and in the community.

Be sure to let families know that their participation is welcome and needed and that you are interested in having them share their expertise as well as their concerns. Family members can be rich resources if they have cultural stories to share, related careers such as plumbing and working with boats, or knowledge about places to visit. Also, encourage family members to work as classroom volunteers. Some families may be able to help in the classroom on a regular basis; others may come in just for special occasions such as field trips or special events. They can serve as invaluable assets when you take the class outdoors, providing children with the adult guidance they need to help them focus on and observe water more deeply. Indoors, family volunteers can assist with small group explorations.

Let parents know what they can do at home with their children. They might explore water together. Suggest different materials and experiences they might share. In addition to playing with water in a bucket or sink, families can explore water outdoors or in the bathtub. Family outings are another great way for children and families to see the science in their communities. Suggest places to go. For example, a trip to a local fountain or waterfall can spark children's curiosity about water flow. Such activities can reinforce and extend the science children are learning in the classroom, while helping children and families see science phenomena in their daily lives. It is also helpful to provide sample questions that families can use to spark children's thinking and questions. "Science Explorations for Families," included in the resources, offers ideas for activities and thoughtful questions that families can ask children. You might also provide families with a list of children's books that relate to the science concepts they are learning. See the "Books and Web Sites" section (p. 105) for some suggestions.

How to Use This Guide

Exploring Water with Young Children includes three stages that will guide you in promoting children's exploration of water and their use of inquiry.

GETTING READY. To facilitate this exploration, you will need to prepare. This section will help you to explore the science concepts embedded in this exploration. This section will also help you prepare the physical environment and think about routines and schedules that support children's inquiry into water.

OPEN EXPLORATION. During this stage, children explore a variety of water materials at the water table and at the water center. These initial explorations are intended to encourage children to find out how they can use the various materials with water and what water does when it's being moved or contained. During this stage, children will also look at books and images of water in different kinds of settings to inspire their water play. This is the time to encourage children to follow their interests and try things out. Resist the temptation to share your own ideas about flow and other properties of water. Instead, encourage children to follow up on their ideas and try new things.

FOCUSED EXPLORATION. After children have had multiple opportunities to openly explore a variety of materials, they are ready for focused exploration. During this stage, you engage children in a deeper exploration of various properties of water. They will have the opportunity to explore water with the help of eyedroppers, boats, and wire and pegboard water walls. Your role is to deepen children's understandings by asking probing questions, encouraging children to represent their work, and creating opportunities for discussion and reflection. Extension activities—such as a field trip to a nearby stream or fountain, the sharing of an interesting book or reference material, or a visit from a plumber—take place about once a week throughout "Focused Exploration." These experiences motivate children to continue their explorations in new ways, provide new information, and/or connect their work to their lives outside of school.

"Focused Exploration" includes three different studies. The flow study helps children look at the ways they can construct water systems through tubes or in streams. The drops study helps children look at the shapes of drops they can make with eyedroppers, and then how those drops compare to drops on different surfaces. The sink and float study encourages children to make "boats" to gain some ideas about sinking and floating.

Each step of "Open Exploration" and "Focused Exploration" includes the following sections:

CORE EXPERIENCES provide a rationale for the step—the science ideas you'll be focusing on, why this is important for children, and how this step relates to the overall exploration.

The **PREPARATION** section will help you get ready for each step as you consider your classroom schedule, the materials you will need, and ways to connect with families.

The **TEACHING PLAN** offers detailed guidance for implementing the step. The left-hand column outlines and guides you through the exploration. Issues teachers have raised and our responses are found in the right-hand column, which also includes photographs, drawings, and sample dialogue. This column gives a picture of what the plan looks like "in action," while suggesting ways to extend science explorations.

The "Teaching Plan" is composed of four parts: "Engage," "Explore," "Extend," and "Reflect." Young children's learning rarely follows a predictable sequence; therefore, these parts can be followed in any order.

- Engage offers suggestions for what you might say and do to encourage children to get excited about and involved in exploring water.

- Explore offers guidance for what you can do to facilitate children's explorations.

- Extend suggests additional teaching strategies (such as using books or photos, going outdoors to observe a particular property of water) to use as a way to enhance children's experiences.

- Reflect suggests different ways to encourage children to discuss the observations they have made and ideas they have begun to form.

At the end of each "Focused Exploration" are three different types of extensions for enriching children's water explorations. They include planning a field trip to explore different environments, inviting experts into the classroom, and using books to extend the exploration.

The resource section provides more information about the teaching approach of *Exploring Water with Young Children*, essential information about where to buy and how to assemble materials, and book and Web resources. We encourage you to familiarize yourself with this section before you start. You will find references to the resources throughout the guide. Some of what is there may be useful to you right away; other material may be more helpful after you have had some initial experiences teaching *Exploring Water with Young Children*.

Lemonade Stand: Excerpts from a Teacher's Journal

These journal entries illustrate what one Head Start teacher learned by involving her class in a study of water.

APRIL 7

Last week I met with the two other teachers who are going to do the exploration, and it was really helpful. Together we played with water using the cups, pumps, tubes, and funnels to explore different ways we could move water. We also thought about our goals, what we expected kids to do, and how our own roles would change over time. And by going through the guide together, it helped us to talk through our questions too.

Now I'm working on my room. I moved the water table so it's right between the bathroom and the kitchen. That will make filling and emptying the table a lot easier. Next I'll put the bins next to the water table to store all the materials—from basters to measuring cups to ladles.

APRIL 12

The kids are really into what they're doing at the water table. While I was observing them, I realized that kids were so much into *doing* that they really didn't pay attention to what was happening when they poured water through the funnel, even when the water squirted out the other end. So now I'm trying to help them notice more by saying things such as, "Hey, look at the tube. Where did the water go? What did it do?" Yeah, they're still into the *doing*, but now they're keeping track of how far the water squirts, noticing more about how what they do affects the distance it travels, and thinking about why.

APRIL 20

The younger kids in my room are not using the tubes, basters, or squirt bottles. They are really excited about using containers and pouring back and forth. I was trying to think of ways to take that further, so I kept asking myself, "What is it that they're trying to figure out here?"

It all seemed to be about the containers and about emptying and filling, so I got different shapes and sizes of containers and put them in the water table. I even spent some time over there and counted out loud as Miguel poured cup after cup into the largest pitcher. Kids are now beginning to discover how one container holds the same amount of water as another container, even though they look different.

APRIL 30

I know we're supposed to have weekly science talks, but it's been a real struggle. The younger kids just roll around on the floor and then the older kids get distracted and we aren't getting anywhere!

So I talked to my supervisor and she gave me some ideas. We even made a plan: first, have shorter science talks until kids are ready for longer ones. She also suggested that I bring concrete reminders of what kids had done with water and the materials they used. I'll keep working on this.

MAY 4

We just finished with a good science talk. Hooray! Most of the kids really listened to one another. Making our talks shorter helped a lot. I've also been bringing the materials that kids used at the water table. With the materials in front of us, kids can show how they used them and what happened to the water. Miguel brought the big pitcher, the measuring cup, and the paper we'd used to tally up the number of cups of water it took to fill the jug. I'm also bringing in pictures of kids using different materials to make water move. With the pictures in front of us, it's so much easier to say, "Tell me what you were doing. What happened when you did that? Why do you think that happened?"

MAY 11

Gabi was trying to get someone to help her with her tubing. She wanted to pour some water into one end but couldn't see it come out the other end because the end was resting in the water, so I held the tube. Then she tried pushing the tube through the grid, but it kept sliding out. She then saw another tube with a T-connector on the end and noticed that it helped to stay in the grid, so she put a connector on the end of hers too.

As she continued to pour the water into the tube and watched it come out one end, Christian picked up a cup and began to catch the water coming out the other end. "Anyone want a drink?" Christian asked. "I got some drinks here!" Gabi laughed and said that this was like the time

we had a lemonade stand. So that's how the idea of having a lemonade stand was born. Gabi poured and Christian "caught" the "lemonade" and served it for a solid thirty minutes, until choice time was over. But Christian and Gabi wanted to continue. So I said I'd take some pictures to help them remember how their lemonade stand looked. They counted the number of funnels and connectors they'd used and asked me to write the numerals on our chart. Finally, they dictated what they were doing so we could continue the investigation next week.

MAY 15

Today we used the photos and our memories to set up the lemonade stand again. While I watched more kids entering this water play, I noticed that the water would only come out in dribbles when the tube was held low. Then when the tube was lifted, the water would come out really fast and the cup would overflow. So I asked all the kids at the lemonade stand what made the water move fast and what made it move slow. Christian said Gabi made it go fast just to bug him. Lynne said it was magic. Something to follow up on.

MAY 18

Today at choice time we read our notes and talked about the flow of water being too fast or too slow. Then Lynne said she didn't think it was magic that made the water fast or slow. She said that Gabi probably did something to make the water go fast or slow without knowing it. So we all watched Gabi pour and Christian catch lemonade. At first, Gabi held the tube down low, and again only dribbles. Then she raised the tubing up high, and the water gushed out all over Christian. Lynne got really excited then, saying, "It was Gabi. She did this!" and she mimicked Gabi holding the tube low, then raising the tube up high. I asked, "Do you mean at first she held the tube down low and the water was slow, but when she lifted it high the water came out fast?" Lynne said yes. I said, "I wonder if we can test that out." So for the rest of choice time, kids tested out Lynne's theory and explored different ways to control the flow of water.

MAY 22

During our science talk, I brought the poster I had made with pictures of the lemonade stand. On the poster, I also recorded kids' ideas about what happened. The children who had created the stand talked about the photos, then shared the different things they tried and discovered about how to make the water go fast and slow. All the kids got really excited and asked if we could have a *real* lemonade stand. I agreed. I wrote down their ideas about what to sell and who would have what jobs. So now we have a flyer maker, a ticket maker, lemonade makers, and someone to collect tickets and serve. We'll need new tubing and connectors to serve real lemonade, and we all agreed they needed to practice controlling the lemonade flow before the big showing.

June 1

All week we've been working on the lemonade stand. Before the big event, we talked about questions that adults and other kids might ask. I wrote all the questions down and the answers that they knew. When we didn't know the answers, I put this in the "Questions to Investigate" column. And so our water investigation continues.

It's funny. I've always had a water table in my room, and it's always been a big draw for the kids. But before, it was mostly about washing the dolls or taking the dinosaurs for a swim. But now the kids are really discovering the science in water as they use the materials to pour, to siphon, to pump—and I'm discovering right alongside them.

References

Carson, Rachel. 1965. *The sense of wonder.* New York: Harper & Row.

Eisenberg, M. 2000. The influence of materials on children's play: Explorations at the water table. Unpublished study, Tufts University.

National Research Council. 1996. *National science education standards.* Washington, D.C.: National Academy Press.

getting ready

Step 1: Preparing Yourself—Science

You interact with water every day—in your kitchen, your bathroom, outside on rainy days. And as a teacher, you probably have spent some time helping children at the sink or water table. But when was the last time you had a chance to sit down and experiment using different types of materials to move and control water, look closely at drops on different surfaces, notice the relationship between air bubbles and water, or make a boat and sail it? Use this section to have experiences with water and develop some basic understandings that prepare you for helping children explore water and its many interesting properties. Collect some of the water exploration materials and bring them, along with a willingness to explore and wonder, to a sink, a water table, or a bucket of water.

TEACHING PLAN

Collect as many of the materials children will use in their exploration of water as possible. A complete list of classroom materials appears below in "Step 3: Preparing the Physical Environment—Materials and Resources."

Place the materials on a counter near a sink. Spend a few minutes pouring water from one empty container into another. Notice and think about the following:

- The height of the water in each container. Before you pour, predict how high the water will go in the new container.

- What water does as it fills a new container.

- How the surface of water looks flat in each container.

- What water looks like when it spills over if there's too much.

- What happens to the air bubbles that may appear, what they look like, and how they behave in the water.

Place the thin end of a funnel into one end of a clear tube.

- Pour water into the funnel, and notice what happens to the water as you do so.

- Try putting your finger or a cork in the other end of the tube. Do you find it is now hard for water to go down the funnel? Why do you think this might be? How can you get water in?

- Take the cork out and turn the tubing into a U shape. What do you notice about the water?

- With the tube still in a U shape, notice whether there are air bubbles in the tubing. What happens to these bubbles as you move the tubing?

- Notice that the top of the water at both ends of the U-shaped tube have a flat surface and are at the same height. When one side of the tube is moved up or down, the water on both sides of the tube remains at the same height.

Straighten the tubing, and place a T- or Y-connector in the open end.

- What happens when you put water into the funnel now?

- What happens when you put your finger over one end of the connector?

- Try connecting several pieces of tubing together directly or with the connectors. Make several combinations of the materials to try to make the water move in a variety of ways.

Place the tip of a turkey baster into a container of water.

- Fill the baster and notice what happens in the container and in the baster as bubbles come out and water goes in.

- Hold the baster up and see whether water comes out. Can you get the water out without squeezing?

- Squirt the water into a container and observe how the water can be forced out of the baster.

- Try adding a piece of clear tubing to the end of the baster. Now what happens when you squeeze the bulb of the baster? Where do you notice air bubbles? What happens when you release the bulb? How can you make water come out of the tubing?

Next, see what it is like to move water with a bilge or kerosene pump. Before you start, what do you think you'll see?

- Place the pump in water and find a way to get the water to move. How does this compare with how water moves with a turkey baster?

- Use the pump to move water from a bucket on the floor to the sink or water table, or use it to empty the water table.

- What do you think is happening inside the pump? If you have a clear pump, what do you see when you look into it? What happens as you pump? What happens as you release the pump?

Move water with other tools.

- Try moving water using a baster and an eyedropper.
- When might you want to use either of them for moving water?

Take a few moments to look at small, thin streams of water. Look at how streams appear when there are holes in the side of a cup, and when they are in the bottom.

- Take two or three clear plastic cups and poke a different-sized hole in the bottom of each. Fill them and watch what happens to the water as it comes out of the hole. Do the streams of water come out through the small holes differently than when they come out the larger holes? When do you see drops, and when do you see a stream?
- Fill clear plastic cups or clear empty plastic bottles that have two or three holes poked in their sides. While you fill, use your fingers or some tape to cover the holes. Take your fingers or the tape away from the holes. What do you notice about the water? What happens to the streams as the water level in the cups goes down?

Explore drops of water. Place a piece of waxed paper on a table or other surface.

- Use an eyedropper to place a drop of water on the waxed paper. Use a hand lens to look closely at the drop. What do you notice about its shape if you look at it from above? From the side?
- Now try to make very large drops. Gradually increase the size of the drops. Is there a point when it no longer seems like a drop?
- Try moving a drop of water along the surface of the waxed paper. What do you notice about how it moves? What do you notice about its shape?
- Do drops of water look the same on other surfaces, such as on the table top? Aluminum foil? A brick? Why do you think they look different?
- What is the difference between a drop and a bubble?

Use objects from around your house or the classroom to find out if they sink or float in a tub or other container of water.

- Before you put the objects in the water, take a careful look at them. What is their shape? What are they made from? Based on your observations, decide whether you think they will sink, float, or hover in the middle when you put them in the tub of water. Can you suggest any patterns or ideas that help to explain why some things float and others sink in water?
- Try floating and sinking a few fruits and vegetables, such as a grape, a lime, a grapefruit, or a carrot. Do the results support your current ideas about what makes something sink or float?

TEACHER NOTE: Adam connected a tube filled with water to make a circle shape, and then laid it on the table.

Adam: *I noticed something about this. When you turn this (the tubing) a little bit, it goes round and round.*

Teacher: *What goes round and round?*

Adam: *The air on top.*

Teacher: *What do you see on the bottom?*

Adam: *The water. (Picks up the tubing and slowly turns it like a steering wheel.) When you go like this, the air goes up here. And you can see the water and the air. See the air? It's making the water go away.*

- Use a walnut-size ball of oil-based clay (such as plasticine) to see if it floats or sinks (it should sink). Try changing the shape of the clay to make it float. Can you change the design yet still keep it afloat? What did you notice about your unsuccessful and successful "boat" designs? Does this information support your ideas about what makes something float or sink?

- Why do you think a piece of paper towel floats at first and then sinks?

As you explored water in different ways with a variety of materials, you engaged in some of the science experiences and concepts children will likely encounter in their exploration of water. Having these experiences yourself will prepare you to act as a guide to children, providing materials, highlighting interesting possibilities, and asking key questions. These experiences also will prepare you for how children are likely to respond to these phenomena.

The following information about the science concepts is *for teacher use only* and is not intended as information for young children.

PROPERTIES OF WATER: WATER FLOWS

Water's movement is generally described as a flow, and water flows down due to gravity. This can be seen in many different ways—rivers flow from higher places to lower ones, drops of rain flow down window panes, streams of rain flow down gutters and downspouts, and water poured slowly from one cup to another will flow to the lower container.

Water can also be made to move up when the force exerted on it is stronger than the downward pull of gravity, such as when you push on it to squirt it up out of a dropper or syringe. Air pressure pushes water up when you squeeze and let go of the bulb on a turkey baster and eyedropper, or when you suck on a straw. Water moves faster or slower depending on the strength of the forces acting on it.

PROPERTIES OF WATER: WATER TAKES THE SHAPE OF ITS CONTAINER

When water is in a cup, a pitcher, a tube, a bowl, a swimming pool, or a lake, the surface of the water will be flat unless it is moved by something else (for example, wind or shaking). All parts of the container will be filled with water.

PROPERTIES OF WATER: COHESION

Water molecules stick together (cohesion). When the amount of the water is small, this property of water causes it to form drops. It is also the cause of *surface tension*, the kind of "skin" on the surface of water. Some bugs, for example, can scoot across the surface of a pond or puddle. If you fill a glass to the very top you can keep adding a small amount until it is actually a little more than full. This is also because of surface tension.

PROPERTIES OF WATER: ADHESION

Water sticks to other materials (adhesion). It sticks more or less strongly depending on what the material is. Water does not stick well

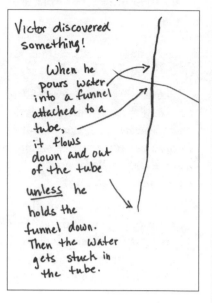

EXAMPLE: This four-year-old's drawing has been annotated by his teacher. It describes his discovery.

Victor discovered something!

When he pours water into a funnel attached to a tube, it flows down and out of the tube unless he holds the funnel down. Then the water gets stuck in the tube.

to waxed paper, so drops are very round—but it sticks well to paper towels or newspapers, so the drops are pulled apart. This property of water is what makes things wet.

PROPERTIES OF OBJECTS IN WATER: OBJECTS CAN SINK, FLOAT, OR STAY SUSPENDED IN WATER

Whether a solid object will sink, float, or stay suspended in water has to do with the relationship between its density and the density of water. Density is the mass of a substance per unit volume; or we can also say it is the weight per unit volume. Some materials will sink in water in one shape and then float if their shape is changed. For example, a ball of clay will sink, whereas that same amount of clay, if spread out and shaped like a boat, will float. The ball of clay is denser than water and sinks. But the boat, made out of the same amount of clay (the same mass), is bigger (more volume). Its density is less than the density of the water it displaces, and it floats. Thus, an ocean liner floats, even though it is made of metal. If we took all that metal and made it into a solid ball, it would certainly sink. There are factors other than shape that also can determine whether an object will sink or float in water. For example, some materials such as Styrofoam or many kinds of wood are less dense than water no matter what their shape. And, some things sink when they are not well balanced because they tip and water comes in.

BEHAVIORS OF AIR IN WATER: AIR TAKES UP SPACE AND AIR BUBBLES FLOAT TO THE TOP OF WATER

Both water and air take up space. In order for water to enter an "empty" cup, funnel, piece of tubing, or turkey baster, it must take the place of the air that was already there. When pouring water into a cup, the air is easily replaced by the water. But if you put a cup under water with its open end down, you have to tip it to let the air out so the water can get into it. You can see the bubbles of air come out. Since air is less dense than water, those bubbles will quickly float to the top of the water, and pop. Sometimes, such as when trying to put water into a narrow piece of tubing that is closed at the bottom, the air in the tubing can't get out the top, allowing no water in.

Step 2: Preparing Yourself—The Guide

This teacher's guide offers detailed, step-by-step guidance on how to prepare and implement each step. Read it through before you begin.

TEACHING PLAN

Read the guide carefully. The left-hand column guides you through the exploration. The right-hand column shows what the plan looks like in action; it contains issues teachers have raised, with corresponding suggestions, photographs, drawings, sample charts, brief dialogue transcripts, and ways you might extend children's science explorations.

TEACHER NOTE: Jasmine was pumping water through a tube, and Diego put his finger over the end of the tube.

Diego: *Look at that! It's spraying like my house.*

Teacher: *Like your house?*

Diego: *Yes, like the yard in my house.*

Teacher: *Do you mean the sprinkler at your house? To water the grass?*

Diego: *Yes, like my house. (Proceeds to "water" various materials in the water table.) Before they put stuff away I asked about sprinklers.*

Teacher: *Where do you think the water comes from? What do you think makes the water come out that way?*

In addition to the step-by-step directions, the guide includes a section of extensions, which has suggestions for planning field trips, inviting experts into the classroom, and using books and Web sites. The resources section provides more information about science teaching, observation and assessment, classroom materials, strategies for involving families, and book and Web site resources.

Step 3: Preparing the Physical Environment—Materials and Resources

Children's learning and excitement will be heightened by the variety and quality of the materials they are able to explore. They will benefit from experiencing materials that contain and move water in different ways and allow them to look more closely at drops, streams, and water flow. They will extend their thinking by having access to a variety of art materials that can be used to represent their experiences, and by looking at books, posters, and photos related to water and boats. Gathering these materials now will help you to provide children with rich opportunities for exploration. In this step you will do the following:

- Prepare the classroom for exploring water.

- Collect materials for the water table and center.

- Collect a variety of art materials.

- Collect water-related books, posters, and photos.

TEACHING PLAN

Use the classroom environment checklist on p. 113 to help you inventory materials, set up your classroom space, and plan your schedule.

1. Collect any large equipment you may not already have.

The water table area should have the following:

- Large water table

- Large tub (approximately 15 by 33 by 6 inches)

The water center should have the following:

- Clear plastic tubs or containers (two or more, approximately 10 by 15 by 6 inches)

It is important to keep the water table open all year. If you do not have a water table in your classroom, borrow one. Water tables are large tables that usually measure about 21 by 45 by 6 inches. If you already have a water table, try to borrow a second one. This allows more children to work at the same time. In addition, it is preferable to have one or more extra tubs at the water table area that are at least 15 by 33 by 6 inches. Having a tub or even a wading pool nearby encourages children to move water back and forth.

"Exploring Water" also takes place in one or more water centers—other areas of the classroom where children will explore smaller quantities of water in smaller tubs and containers, either on tables or the floor. See "Essential Information" on p. 101 of the resources section for further information about the materials used in the exploration.

2. Collect basic materials for children to use throughout the exploration.

   The suggested quantities are for six children. Borrow materials from other classrooms, if necessary.

   - Long-sleeved water smocks (at least six)

   - Clear plastic containers for pouring and containing water (at least twelve); containers in a variety of shapes and sizes (such as tall and narrow, tall and wide, short and narrow, short and wide), and, if possible, square or rectangular containers as well as round ones. Some containers can have visible lines for measurement (such as measuring cups or spoons)

   - Turkey basters (at least six)

   - Clear flexible tubing (at least three pieces) ³⁄₁₆-inch inside diameter (ID) and ⁵⁄₁₆-inch outside diameter (OD) cut into 1-, 2-, and 3-foot lengths

   - Clear flexible tubing (at least three pieces) ³⁄₈-inch ID and ½-inch OD cut into 1-, 2-, and 3-foot lengths

   - Clear flexible tubing (at least three pieces) ½-inch ID cut into 1-, 2-, and 3-foot lengths

   - Funnels (at least six, and two of each size) that fit snugly into the different sizes of tubing

   - Tube connectors—three T- and three Y-shaped connectors to fit into ³⁄₁₆-inch, ³⁄₈-inch, and ½-inch ID flexible tubing

   - Clear plastic squirt bottles (six or more; empty dish soap or shampoo bottles work well)

3. Collect materials for the focused exploration of flow

   - Materials for constructing a wire water wall (For more information, see "Essential Information" on p. 103 of the resources section regarding materials used.)
     - Plastic-coated closet shelving (one piece; at least 15 inches wide, cut to fit inside a water table)
     - Small (12- to 15-inch) pieces of shelving to act as "legs" for the wall (at least two pieces)

   - Pumps
     - Bilge pump
     - Kerosene pumps (at least two)
     - Pumps from bottles of soap or lotion (two or more)

TEACHER NOTE: Water tables and tubs should be emptied and sanitized, along with water play materials, daily. The National Health and Safety Performance Standards recommend using a solution of ¼ cup bleach to 1 gallon of water to cover water play materials and surfaces. They also recommend letting the bleach solution sit for two minutes before it is wiped off.

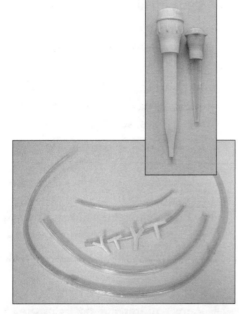

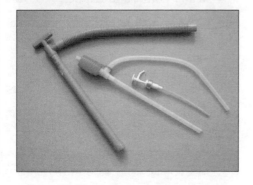

4. Collect materials for the focused exploration of streams.

   • Sixteen or more empty clear plastic water bottles,
     8 ounces or larger (For more information, see "Essential Informa-
     tion" on p. 103 of the resources section.)

   • Materials for a Velcro pegboard (For a full description, see p. 103.)
     – Pegboard (one piece of ¼-inch thick; approximately 2 by 4
       feet)
     – Rough-sided waterproof Velcro (4 yards of 4-inch wide)
     – Fuzzy-sided waterproof Velcro (1 yard of 1-inch wide)

5. Collect materials for the focused exploration of drops.

   • Plastic eyedroppers (at least six)

   • White rigid plastic plates (at least six)

   • Other surfaces on which to explore drops: waxed paper,
     aluminum foil, other papers, fabric scraps

6. Collect materials for the focused exploration of sinking and floating.

   • Six rigid tubes (For information about purchasing and cutting
     these tubes, see p. 102.)

   • Materials for making boats
     – Clean, empty yogurt containers
     – Styrofoam meat trays that have been washed with very hot,
       soapy water
     – Pieces of corrugated and shirt-weight cardboard
     – Cardboard rolls from paper towels
     – Aluminum foil
     – Straws
     – Different kinds of paper

   • Items children can use as cargo: toy cars, people, animals, or
     math manipulatives

7. Collect as many of the following materials as possible for children
   to use to represent their water explorations. Borrow materials from
   other classrooms, if necessary.

   • Markers, crayons, and pencils

   • Clipboards that can be managed by young children (or card-
     board with a bulldog clip attached)

   • Water colors and tempera

   • Collage materials that can represent water materials (such as
     small cups, toilet paper rolls, blue yarn, blue tissue paper, pipe
     cleaners)

8. Collect other water-related resources.

   • Books about water, plumbing, rivers, waterfalls, and boats

   • Posters, old calendars, and photos of waterfalls, boats, white-
     water rapids, or fountains (See "Books and Web Sites" on p. 105
     of the resources section for specific suggestions.)

Step 4: Preparing the Physical Environment—Classroom Setup

Your classroom setup makes a statement about the importance of water exploration when it provides ample space for water play, related displays, and large group science talks.

TEACHING PLAN

1. Organize your classroom to provide children with the following:

   - A water play area that can accommodate five or six children

   To accommodate more children at once, set up one water table and a large tub or container of water on a different table or the floor; or try to borrow a second water table.

   - One or two water centers (small tables or sections of the floor) where children can explore water in clear plastic tubs or containers

   Choose tables or floor areas that are not in the middle of classroom traffic.

   If you have a sink in your classroom, put the water table and water centers near the sink. You might have to dismantle a section of your classroom temporarily to make room for the water centers during *Exploring Water with Young Children.* Make room around your water tables and water centers for children to move freely.

2. Create a space for children to hang up wet water smocks and to store dry clothes.

3. Create a place to store old newspaper, paper or cloth towels, sponges, and a mop.

4. Organize your classroom display spaces to provide children with the following:

   - Wall space at children's eye level on which to hang their drawings and paintings, as well as pictures or posters of interesting water images

   - A selection of books related to rivers, waterfalls, boats, plumbing, and fountains (see "Books and Web sites," p. 105)

5. Create a meeting space large enough for all of your children and their teachers to sit in an open circle for science talks.

Step 5: Long-Term Planning

Exploring Water with Young Children is not a theme or activity-based curriculum but rather a science inquiry that develops over time. It involves children's engagement at the water table, but it is different from simply having the water table available for choice time. The more time children have to explore water with a variety of materials and reflect on their experiences, the more they will get out of the study. However, it does not assume that all children spend all of their time engaged in water play. Your children will have time to engage in play and reflection that are not focused on water, even as the *Exploring Water with Young Children* inquiry continues. Here are some suggestions for things to think about as you plan this study:

- Keep the water areas open at least four days per week for forty-five minutes or longer. The more opportunities children have to explore water with the various materials, the more experiences they will have with the science of water.

- Conduct a whole-group science talk once a week. When children are first introduced to science talks, the discussions can last just five minutes. As the study progresses, children become accustomed to the format and science talks will get longer.

- Open explorations at the water centers last for a few weeks. It takes time for children to learn new routines and to develop an interest in a focused exploration.

- During focused exploration, children may be focusing on different properties of water at the water table and at the water center. For example, as children focus on drops or sinking and floating at the water center(s), they continue to explore water flow or streams at the water table. When they sink and float objects at the water center, they build and test boats at the water table.

Step 6: Classroom Schedule and Routines

Children need time to explore water. You may need to adjust your schedule for this exploration to give them that time. And water exploration can worry teachers and families: children can get wet, floors can get slippery, and water can get dirty. By planning ahead, choosing materials that help to keep children and floors dry, and choosing equipment that allows you to fill and empty water tables efficiently and keep them clean, you can avoid some of these worries. Establish simple rules and routines for yourself and the children so that the time is well used.

Teaching Plan

1. Review your schedule. Make time for the following:

- 45–60 minutes of choice time, at least three times per week (Be sure to have the water table and water centers open during these times.)

TEACHER NOTE: Daire was able to make a ping-pong ball move up a gutter attached to the wire water wall. He was very proud and wanted to share his discovery with the whole group. I drew the wire water wall setup and the gutters, and he drew the ping-pong ball and the water flow. I thought he was ready to think about using arrows to show movement.

Teacher: *When I look at our drawing of the ball in the gutter of water, I can't tell which way the water's going. How can we let the other children know which way the water was flowing?*

Daire: *With the ball, you could use arrows.*

Teacher: *That would help! Show me. Now, what about the moving water?*

TEACHER NOTE: Not only did my children want to create rules for water play, but they also wanted to write them down themselves. They have really taken ownership for their behavior.

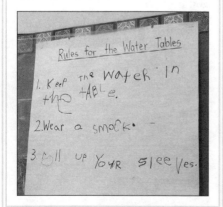

- 10–15 minutes for a meeting with the whole group, at least once per week

2. Review your procedures for choice time.

- Be sure that your procedures allow children to return to explore water on consecutive days so they can continue their work.

- Consider ways, if possible, to allow connected tube setups to remain standing from one day to the next so that children have the opportunity to sustain a water-flow project.

3. Plan a way to fill, empty, and clean water tables.

- To fill water tables, try attaching a large funnel to a piece of clear tubing that is long enough to reach from the sink's faucet to the water tables. Or, plan to fill buckets and carry them, or roll them on a cart, to the water tables and centers.

- Use a bilge pump attached to a piece of clear tubing to empty most of the water from the table. Use large sponges to remove the remaining water. Prepare a spray bottle of 1 tablespoon bleach to 1 gallon cool water, and clean the bottom and sides of the water tables each day after you empty them.

4. Prepare the floor under the water tables to prevent children and teachers from slipping on spilled water.

- If your water tables have to be on a carpeted area, you may want to get a large piece of heavy plastic to put under them, and then cover the plastic with a large cloth, towels, or newspapers.

- If your water tables can be on an uncarpeted area of the classroom, try putting newspapers, towels, or rubber mats under the table. You can use rubber bath mats or squares of rubber matting that fit together and are sold at home improvement stores.

5. Keep everything you and the children are likely to need nearby.

- Put large plastic tubs to store the water materials under the water tables, or make shelves available nearby, so children can take them out and put them away easily.

- Keep a pile of newspaper, cloth towels, sponges, and a small mop (if possible, cut the handle down by half) near the water tables or centers.

- Collect extra sets of dry clothing.

- Plan to put trays or shallow tubs under each container at the center(s) to collect spills.

6. Review your safety rules and procedures for clean-up time. Be sure children are clear about the following:

- The maximum number of children who can be at each water table or center for a given time

- Procedures for sharing materials

TEACHER NOTE: My children love filling and emptying the water table each day.

- Procedures for putting materials away

- Procedures for draining the water table or other containers

- Procedures for drying the floor

- Not putting any materials, including clear tubing,
  into their mouths

Step 7: Families

By the time they start your class, children have already had many opportunities to play with and explore water. Some families, however,
may have concerns about safety and the value of water play. Connecting with families as you get started will allow you to alleviate concerns and articulate the goals of your program. It can also help you
find out about and build on children's life experiences, use family resources, and make suggestions for how families can support children's
water explorations at home and in the community.

TEACHING PLAN

Send a letter to families that describes the important science understandings children will develop as they focus on exploring water with
a variety of materials, and suggest ways that families can support children's science learning. There is a sample letter to families on p. 106
in the resources section; you can adapt it to fit your circumstances
and your families. Also, provide families with tips for exploring water
with their children by sending home the "Families Exploring Water"
handout on p. 107. Preview the suggestions described in the "Connecting with Families" sections at the beginning of each step of open
and focused exploration in the teacher's guide for specific ways you
can partner with families around their children's science learning.

- Find out who might volunteer or who has skills and experience
  (such as plumbers and water engineers) to share with the class.

- Make a list of ways families can help in the classroom. You might
  want to post this list in the classroom so families are reminded
  that their help is welcome.

- Set up a bulletin board where family members can see examples
  of their children's work and photos of their water explorations.

- Anticipate and address concerns families may have about their
  children's involvement in water play. There are generally two
  kinds of concerns: health (children being wet, especially in cold
  weather), and learning (children are "just playing"). Health concerns can be addressed by having an extra set of dry clothing on
  hand for each child. Learning concerns can be addressed
  through the following event.

- Plan and hold a family science event where families can explore
  the materials and where you can explain the goals of the water
  exploration.

open exploration

Step 1: Introduce Children to Exploring Water

Three- to five-year-olds have been exploring water all their lives, whether in the bath, at a sink, in the rain, or on a beach. Ideally they have had regular opportunities to explore at the water table area in your classroom too. This open exploration of water builds on children's prior experiences by giving them plenty of time to explore water with materials selected to highlight water's movement and its ability to take the shape of its container. In addition, open exploration introduces children to science talks with the whole class, which continue throughout open and focused explorations. Science talks give children opportunities to reflect on their observations, experiences, questions, and theories, and they create a group sense of shared purpose and excitement. This initial step helps you set the tone for an exciting and manageable water exploration. It guides your thoughtful introduction of new materials, rules, and routines, and it introduces you to some of the strategies and roles you will be using throughout *Exploring Water with Young Children*.

CORE EXPERIENCES

☐ Share prior experiences with water.

☐ Hear about materials in various water centers.

☐ Explore water and water materials.

☐ Share current experiences with water.

TEACHER NOTE: martin showed us how he made water come out of the end of a long tube by attaching a funnel to one end. He didn't say anything about his exploration; he just wanted to show us what happened.

Preparation

- ☐ Set up the water table area and a water center. (See p. 18 in "Getting Ready" for detailed information.)

- ☐ Display books and posters about water in "dry" locations around the room.

- ☐ Read the section on science teaching (pp. 95–99) for information about young children's inquiry and for strategies you can use to engage children in the exploration.

- ☐ Collect a small container of water, two different sizes of cups or containers, and a funnel to bring to the initial meeting with the whole class.

- ☐ Make a few copies of the observation record form, p. 116.

Schedule

Set the schedule for the next week, or until all interested children have explored with the new materials. Include the following:

- ☐ 10–15 minutes for an introductory meeting with the whole class

- ☐ 45–60 minutes for choice time, four or five times during the week

- ☐ 10–15 minutes for discussion with the whole class

Materials

One set for the Water Table and another set for the Water Center(s)

- ☐ 3 or more long-sleeved water smocks

- ☐ 6 or more clear plastic containers, including measuring cups

- ☐ 12 pieces of clear tubing in three different diameter sizes, cut into 1-, 2-, and 3-foot lengths

- ☐ 3 or more clear plastic funnels that fit snugly into the various sizes of tubing

Family Connection

- ☐ Send home a note that introduces the "Exploring Water" study and that suggests ways families might help. (See p. 106 for a sample letter.)

- ☐ Schedule and plan an evening when parents and other family members can meet in the classroom, explore water with a range of materials, or talk about ways you can work together to support the study of water in and out of school.

Teacher note: I've taped a shower curtain to the floor under the water table, and I've found two big bins for children to keep materials in, under the table. We have a clothesline for hanging wet towels and water smocks, which are kitchen garbage bags with holes for heads and arms.

See p. 18 in step 3 of "Getting Ready" for specific information about these materials.

Issue: *I feel uneasy about having water in tubs at a table. Even at the water table there are always spills.*

Response: Water play at a water table is about small amounts of water and focused attention on a few materials and properties of water. Some ways to prevent water from getting on the floor are covering tables with layers of newspaper, putting tubs of water on trays to catch spills, and filling tubs only 3 or 4 inches full of water.

TEACHING PLAN

ENGAGE

Lead a discussion with the whole group, lasting five to ten minutes, to introduce "Exploring Water."

Discuss children's previous experiences with water.

When you start the exploration, gather the children together in a circle and invite them to share experiences they've had playing with water. Begin by sharing one of your own experiences. For example, you might say something like this:

- *When I make vegetable soup I like to see which veggies sink and which ones float. And sometimes I pretend the carrots are boats and I watch them sail around inside my sink.*

- *Where do you play with water? The bathtub, sink, puddle, a stream?*

- *What do you do? What do you play with?*

Encourage all children to contribute by asking questions such as the following:

- *Who else likes to (watch sticks float down a stream, play with boats in the bathtub, splash in puddles)? What happens when you do that?*

Introduce new materials.

Tell the children that the class is going to really explore water and that's why you've rearranged the water table area, cleared a new space in the room for a water center, and have new materials for them to use in their water play.

Show children a funnel and a piece of tubing. Invite them to tell about times they've used or seen funnels or tubing. Ask questions such as: "What were they used for?" Then invite children to share ideas they have for using the funnels and tubing in their water play. Perhaps your children will want to hold and position the materials as they share their ideas.

Discuss rules and routines.

Tell children that both the water table and the water center will be open during choice times for many weeks and they will have lots of time to play with the new materials.

Ask the children to help you make a list of things they can do to keep their classroom and the people in it as dry as possible. Record their ideas on a chart. Demonstrate the particular ways you would like children to do the following:

- Put smocks on, take them off, and hang them up.
- Clean up spills with a mop, towels, or sponges.
- Fill and empty the water table each day.

ISSUE: *My children have a difficult time sitting through discussions. What can I do?*

RESPONSE: Teachers find they are able to build children's interest in science talks by beginning with short meetings lasting four or five minutes. They also suggest engaging the children with an object, photograph, or drawing to focus the talk.

Sharing what children notice about water offers them opportunities to develop their descriptive language. Throughout this exploration, use vocabulary that describes the movement of water, the sounds it makes, the way objects behave in it, how it behaves on different materials, and so on. In addition to modeling descriptive vocabulary, help children refine their descriptions by asking questions such as the following:

- How did the stream change?

- How much of the boat was under water?

- How is this drop different from that one?

TEACHER NOTE: Holly was captivated with the way water traveled down the funnel.

As you transition children to choice time, focus the children going to the water table and water center on their new exploration by saying something such as the following:

- *I can't wait to find out what the water does when you use the funnels and tubing!*

EXPLORE

Use tubing, funnels, and various containers to explore water during choice times, until all interested children have participated.

Observe and document children's water explorations.

Spend a few minutes observing children as they engage in water play.

Make sketches or take photos of how children use the materials. Use an observation record form to note what children are doing and what they are noticing. Observe the following:

- What are they noticing as they fill and empty containers? The weight of the water? The way it spills over the top?
- What are they doing with the tubes? How are they filling them with water?
- How are they using the funnel?
- How are they combining the materials?
- What kinds of play are children engaged in?
  - Exploratory: trying out the materials to see what they do
  - Dramatic: using the materials as part of a dramatic play scenario such as "gas station"
  - Constructive: using the materials to build something, such as a fountain (For example, are the children using the materials to invent a game to see how fast they can empty a tub?)

Use these notes to facilitate the upcoming science talk.

Acknowledge children's exploration.

Children who are actively exploring water should be left to play. However, as you observe children's exploration, you can support their work by acknowledging them with a smile, or taking a photograph of them as they work. You might also spend a few minutes modeling water play by exploring water yourself. As you do so, children are likely to join you or invite you into their play.

Some children appreciate when adults acknowledge their work with a comment or a conversation. When children ask if you would like to drink some of their secret lemonade, for example, ask how they made it. Or, if children want to show you something they are doing, ask them to tell you about it.

TEACHER NOTE: I decided to write on my calendar specific times when I would observe children's water explorations. This kind of planning also helped my assistant know when she would have to be in charge.

ISSUE: *I'm not a very good artist. Why should I sketch what the children are doing?*

RESPONSE: Taking the time to sketch children's water systems is a way of acknowledging the importance of what children are doing. Another purpose is to provide an outline of the materials so that children can show you how water has moved through the materials. Simple line drawings of funnels (triangles) and tubes (lines) can be a good starting point for a discussion about water flow.

TEACHER NOTE: If I hadn't spent time watching the children explore I never would have noticed their fascination with trying to fill containers up to the very top without spilling.

Encourage all children to explore the new materials.

Suggest ideas that appeal to a child's special interest. For example, if a child likes dramatic play in the kitchen, invite him to come to the water area to make a beverage or food he might need or use in the kitchen.

Invite a child to play with someone who is enthusiastic about water, or to play with you.

REFLECT

Share and discuss observations with small groups at both the water table and water center near the end of choice time, and in a science talk with the whole group.

Conduct discussions with small groups during choice time.

Near the end of choice time, ask children at the water table to show you some of what they have been doing with the materials. Encourage them to describe what happened to the water by asking questions such as the following:

- *Can you show us how you got water into the tube?*
- *What happened to the water when you put it in the funnel?*

Conduct a large group science talk.

Gather your whole group together in a circle and initiate a science talk by using one of the following strategies:

- Show one or two pieces of equipment.
- Share a photograph or sketch from the exploration.
- Share an observation you made of a child using a funnel or tubing.

Use follow-up questions such as the following to extend the conversation:

- *Did anyone else try something like what Eli did? What happened when you put water in the tubing?*
- *Who used the funnel? What happened to the water? Did anyone have something different happen when they used a funnel? Tell us about it.*

ISSUE: *My children cannot sit and discuss things in a large group.*

RESPONSE: It is important for children to learn to share their experiences and ideas with the group, to listen to others' ideas, and to question and discuss. These are important skills for learning science. You can help children build these skills over time. Begin with short discussions. Take time to encourage sharing and talk about how well children listen.

Teacher: *I noticed John using the funnel. What happened when you used the funnel, John?*

John: *Water fall down.*

Teacher: *Can you show us with this funnel? Use your finger to show us what the water did. Do you think you might be able to make the water fall up?*

John: *(Turns the funnel upside down.)*

Teacher: *So, you're thinking that if you hold the funnel upside down, then the water would fall up. Show us with your finger what the water would do. Oh! So you're thinking that you could pour the water into the big part of the funnel that's now on the bottom and the water might shoot out the little part that's now pointed up? What do the rest of you think? What do you think will happen if John pours water into the funnel when it's like this?*

Step 2: Ongoing Open Exploration

Initial explorations with water will be exciting for most children. As they continue to explore the water centers with a changing array of materials, children will go beyond their initial excitement and begin to explore more questions and develop some ideas about properties of water that will help them move toward more focused explorations.

Core Experiences

☐ Continue to explore water with clear plastic containers, funnels, tubing, and syringes.

☐ Explore water with plastic squirt bottles and basters.

☐ Discuss experiences with water at the water table and the water center(s).

☐ Think about and look for water in books and in daily life.

Preparation

Photocopy the observation record form.

Schedule

Set the schedule for the week, or until all children have participated in the following:

☐ 5–10 minutes for a meeting before each choice time

☐ 45–60 minutes for choice time, four or five times during the week

☐ 5–10 minutes for discussions with the whole group, once a week

Materials

At the Water Table

Add a set of the following to materials already at the water table and water center(s):

☐ 3 or more plastic turkey basters

☐ 3 or more clear plastic squirt bottles

Family Connection

☐ Send notes home periodically detailing what children are doing and learning.

☐ Encourage family members to work with you in the classroom. Prepare a brief explanation of what they can do to facilitate children's water exploration or to give you time to observe and encourage the water exploration.

☐ Create a sign-out sheet for families interested in borrowing water exploration materials over a weekend.

Teacher note: I shared a photo of Monica, Isabel, and Marissa pouring water from one large container into another, and we had the following conversation:

Teacher: *What can you tell me about the water you were pouring?*

Marissa: *It can spill. I like the way it spills on the sides when it gets full.*

Monica: *It can get all wet. I got my shirt wet. The floor got wet, but I cleaned it up.*

Teacher: *Who else has been pouring water at the water center? What did you notice?*

Early on I decided not to use the basters because I was certain that children would use them to just squirt each other. But another teacher in the workshop we're attending convinced me to try. She said she'd talked to each group that chose to explore water about checking to see where the tips of their basters were pointing before they squeezed. I tried the same thing, and it worked! A few kids did squirt each other, but I used it as an opportunity to talk with them about how to predict where the water will go before they squirt.

TEACHING PLAN

ENGAGE

Allow five to ten minutes during a meeting with the whole group to discuss the ongoing open exploration.

Introduce materials that squirt water.

Introduce basters and squirt bottles during a meeting with the whole group before choice time.

Show children a baster and invite them to share their experiences with basters or their ideas about what they might be for.

Do the same with a squirt bottle, or wait and introduce them on another day.

Tell the children that these materials have been added to the materials already at the water table and the water center.

Facilitate a conversation about children's experiences with these materials by asking questions such as the following:

- *What do you think you might do with a baster at the water table?*
- *How do you think basters work?*

Talk with children about developing rules and safe practices for using basters and squirt bottles, and post these rules in the water center.

Invite advanced water explorers to share their experiences.

Encourage children's continued exploration of water flow and motivate all children to participate in the exploration by focusing the group on recent events at the water table. Provide children with concrete reminders—such as your sketches or photographs, or materials from the water table—to help them recall and share their experiences more easily. Ask questions like these:

- *What did you do at the water table yesterday?*
- *How have you been getting water into the tubing?*
- *What happened when you put the funnel into the tubing?*

EXPLORE

Encourage children's exploration during choice time until all children have participated.

Observe and document children's exploration.

Spend a few minutes observing children as they engage in water play. You might do any of these things:

- Make sketches or take photographs of how children use the materials.
- Use the observation form to record what children do and say. Look for the following:

ISSUE: *Should I teach my children how to use a baster?*

RESPONSE: Problem solving and persistence are important skills and attitudes for children to develop. Don't jump in too soon. But if a child is becoming frustrated, encourage children who have figured out how to work with basters to help those who haven't. If no one knows how to use one, show one or two children and let them show the others.

TEACHER NOTE: Zack drew this picture and told me, "I liked to play in the water. It went down to the other water. I poured it in and it went around and around. And I stirred it and I made magic."

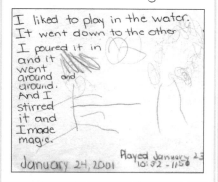

I liked to play in the water. It went down to the other I poured it in and it went around and around. And I stirred it and I made magic.

January 24, 2001   Played January 23 10:32 - 11:50

ISSUE: *The water table looks so crowded with materials right now. Should I put some away?*

RESPONSE: Too many materials in the water at once can be overwhelming. But children need access to a range of materials. Try keeping bins under the water table for storing materials so children have easy access to them and so that all of the materials are not in the water table.

- How are they using the basters and squirt bottles?
- How are they filling them with water?

- How are they combining the materials?

- Do they notice bubbles and how they move? Do they notice where bubbles come from?

- What kind of play are children engaged in?
  - Exploratory: trying out the materials to see what they do.
  - Dramatic: using the materials as part of a dramatic play scenario such as "hospital."
  - Constructive: using the materials to build something, such as a fountain. For example, are the children using the materials to invent a game to see how far they can squirt water?

Use your photographs, sketches, and notes about children's experiences and ideas to create a documentation panel. The documentation panel communicates to children and adults how children have been using materials at the water table and at the water center(s) to explore water. See guidelines for creating documentation panels on p. 115. The panel can be used during an upcoming science talk and as a way to talk with parents about children's science inquiry.

Acknowledge children's ongoing explorations.

As you observe children's explorations, acknowledge their work with descriptions of the effects their use of the materials have on water. For example, you might make comments like these:

- *When you squeezed the baster into the tube, water came out this end.*

- *You made bubbles when you squeezed the squirt bottle under water.*

If children engage you in conversation, ask questions that focus on the water they are moving:

- *Where is it going?*

- *What's happening to the bubbles?*

- *What are you using the funnel, baster, or tubing for?*

Offer interested children clipboards, paper, and pencils or markers so they can draw their experiences. Children who see you making sketches of their exploration will be more likely to want to try sketching themselves.

Encourage all children to participate.

Use strategies such as the following to be sure all children have opportunities to explore water with these materials. Their common experiences build the foundation upon which focused explorations are built.

- Assign reluctant children to the water table or the water center with a few enthusiastic explorers during choice time.

TEACHER NOTE: Today was the first day children noticed bubbles at the water table. They asked me if I'd put soap in the water. When I told them I hadn't, they started mixing the water around with their hands and created more bubbles. I'm going to remind them of their experience and facilitate a science talk focused on their ideas about bubbles!

TEACHER NOTE: Valda was fascinated by the bubbles escaping from the funnel she'd inverted and placed in the tub of water. When I asked her where she thought the bubbles were coming from, she lifted up the funnel a pinch and looked under it. "Can you make more?" I asked. She proceeded to repeatedly lift the funnel up and down, and Nina called it a bubble machine.

- Invite reluctant explorers to hold a tube or funnel for you or one of their friends.

- Place an "observer's chair" near the water table for children who may want to watch the water play for a day or two before they join in. Engage the observer with comments about what's happening at the water table. For example: "Wow! Did you see that? They made the water come out of that tube like a faucet. I wonder how they did that."

EXTEND

Look at books about water.

Use one or two pages from books with large photographs or drawings of water to help individuals, small groups, or your whole group of children reflect on their open exploration. Ask children to compare what they've experienced with water with what they see in the photographs. Ask follow-up questions like these:

- *What do you notice about how the water seems to be moving in this picture? Have you done anything like that with water?*

- *Look at how the illustrator drew the shape of the water in this picture. Have you ever seen water look like that?*

Look at moving water outdoors.

Tell children that during choice time you will take turns bringing small groups of children for a walk around the school building (or outside if it is raining or has rained recently) so they can look for water. Remind children that water can be found in many different places. You might ask questions like these:

- *Where do you think we'll see water?*

- *What do you think it will look like?*

- *Where do you think we will find puddles? Drips? Streams?*

Bring a camera, if possible, and clipboards with paper and markers attached. If it's safe to do so, have children sit and draw what they see when they find pipes or evidence of water. Outside, invite children to sit and draw a roof, gutters, and downspouts.

REFLECT AND DISCUSS

With small groups during choice time, and in weekly science talks with the whole group for ten to fifteen minutes, share water play experiences.

Conduct small group discussions during choice time.

Every couple of days, join children at the water table or the water center for a few minutes before choice time ends. Ask children to tell you about their play and use follow-up questions like these to focus their thinking on the effects their use of materials has on water.

ISSUE: *My children are always splashing each other.*

RESPONSE: Controlling water is not easy for young children. Unexpected splashes will happen. But if children are purposefully splashing each other, you need to reiterate clear rules, redirect their play, and, as a last resort, remove children from the area for the day if they cannot or will not stop.

TEACHER NOTE: Summer loves the water table and the collage table. After she'd observed bubbles one day and I'd printed some photos of her exploration, I engaged her at the collage table. She used our photos to make a three-dimensional representation of her discovery. Then I asked her if she would draw me a picture of what happened. She agreed! As she told me about her drawing, I wrote down her words: "I took the cup and screwed the cover on it and I scooped up the water with a shovel into the cup, all the way to the top of the cup. I put a funnel in the hole and tipped it over slowly. The water came out. There were bubbles inside the cup while the water was coming out."

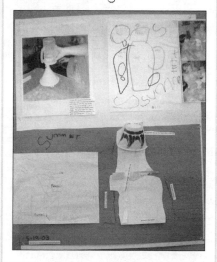

- *What happened when you lifted the funnel up? Put the end of the tube in the baster? Squeezed the squirt bottle under water?*

- *What did it look like? What did you notice about what happened to the water?*

- *Did the same thing happen to anyone else? How was your experience different?*

Conduct weekly science talks with the whole group.

Use your sketches or photos of children's exploration to initiate a conversation about what children are noticing.

You might ask or say something like this:

- *Justicia, what were you doing in this picture? Where did the water go? How did you help it to get there?*

Invite children to compare experiences. You might say something like this:

- *Who else used the squirt bottles? Tell us about it.*

- *Did anyone else discover the bubbles coming out of the baster? Tell us what you noticed.*

Transition from Open Exploration to Focused Exploration

When children are engaged in open exploration, they notice, wonder, and ask general questions about water. Children's questions are expressed in actions and words. For example, during open exploration, a child may reach for a funnel to fill a tube. Or a child might say, "Let's use this baster to squirt the water up."

During a focused exploration, children plan an investigation that focuses on a question that is central to their particular interest. They make new observations and record and represent their experiences. They reflect on their actions and look for patterns and relationships. Often these reflections lead them to ask new questions. These experiences can also lead to the formulation of new understandings or theories based on the evidence they have gathered.

When children begin to focus their observations and ask specific questions about how water behaves, they may be ready for focused exploration. Here are some samples of more specific questions children may begin to ask: Will this skinny tube move water faster than this fatter one? Do drops always run down? How can I get water to move up? Do all heavy things sink?

If most of your children have been engaged in water play a number of times over the past few weeks, many of them may have developed a particular interest. Here are some signs to look for to determine which children might like to pursue a more focused question or exploration:

TEACHER NOTE: Yesterday Reggie and Rey played gas station at the water table. Empty bottles became cars, and they filled the cars up with gas by putting hoses into the bottles and pouring water into the other end of the hose. I jotted down the pieces of their conversation that related to their experiences controlling the flow of the gas, and I took a few photographs too. During today's science talk I invited the two boys to talk about the photos, and I read aloud a transcript of their conversation.

> **Reggie:** *The gas is spilling—it's spilling! Hey, you can't spill the gas! I'll get a bigger car. Look! It's going in, but you have to go faster. Go faster!*
>
> **Rey:** *I'm going fast! The gas goes slow. I have to stop to fill up the pumper.*
>
> **Reggie:** *Let me do it. Let me go faster. This goes too slow. Pour it with something else.*

The boys told us that the gas didn't get into the cars very well—it spilled, and it went slow, and then stopped. I asked the group to help make a list of things the boys might do to keep the gas from spilling and to help it move faster. We posted the finished list next to the water table:

- Use a funnel at the end of the tube and then pour the gas.

- Use a baster to squirt the gas into the cars.

- Shake the gas when it's in the tube and get it to go in the car.

I'll refer to the list for the next few days as children explore the suggestions.

- Spending a full choice time interacting with water in purposeful ways. These children often have ideas in mind about what they want to do. They may be continuing play from the previous day or exploring what materials can do to move or contain water.

- Becoming more deliberate in how they explore water. For example, as children pour water from one container to another, they begin to shift their focus from less controlled pouring between containers to more careful pouring.

- Not choosing the water table or a water center any longer after having been involved previously.

Children took the lead during open exploration, following their interests using a number of different materials. Your role as teacher was to reflect on what you observed children doing, to determine what they were trying to do and wanted to know, and to support and encourage their work. Open exploration was also the time to learn what your children seemed most interested in as they explored water. In focused exploration, children will still take the lead, but you will play a greater role: you will gather resources and background information, create opportunities for children to look more carefully and learn more deeply, and challenge them to go further and think more deeply about their experiences.

Focused exploration includes three different studies that can occur in any order and often simultaneously. The flow study focuses children on beginning to develop theories about how and why what they do makes water move in particular ways. This study relies on materials and setups that provoke children to move water in various ways and reflect on what they do to control that movement. The drops study helps children begin to develop two additional important concepts: water sticks to itself (cohesion) and water sticks more or less strongly to different materials (adhesion). This study relies on children's careful observation of drops; they focus on the shape and movement of drops and how those shapes and movements differ when drops are on various materials. The sinking and floating study focuses on helping children begin to notice that objects sink or float in water depending on a number of factors including their shape, what's inside them, and what they're made from. This study supports children as they collect data and develop theories about why some objects sink and others float.

You may notice that some of your children will remain engaged in open exploration and might want to continue to pour water from container to container; this is fine. They can continue with open exploration while others shift to focused exploration. Participating in the group discussions, observing, and listening to the children who are focusing on particular properties of water more closely will help those in open exploration become interested in more focused questions. Most children, however, move back and forth between open and focused exploration. The transition is not one-way; rather, it is cyclical. In focused exploration, when children are introduced to a

TEACHER NOTE: Beth told us that she was trying to get water to go through the tube in the funnel. She said she tried putting water in the funnel but it didn't get into the tube, so she put the tube under the water and got some in that way.

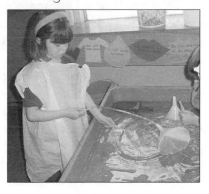

EXAMPLE: These children enjoyed filling the baster and squirt bottle and then seeing how fast they could make the water come out.

new challenge or a new material, they may return to open exploration in order to become more familiar with these new things before shifting back to focused exploration.

FOCUSED EXPLORATION: FLOW, DROPS, SINK AND FLOAT

Children have been using a variety of materials as part of their water play. They have had opportunities to notice how those materials move water, how they either sink or float in water, how water drops look and move differently on materials with different textures, and how water fills containers of various shapes and sizes. You have observed their play and have encouraged them to share their experiences with these materials.

Now, by introducing new materials to children's water play, you focus their exploration more narrowly. Bottles and cups with holes punched in them invite children to notice streams and to do so more closely; eyedroppers, hand lenses, and different kinds of fabrics, papers, and other materials encourage children to explore cohesion and adhesion; boat-building materials and a good variety of objects to place in tubs full of water will focus children on sinking and floating; and shelves in the water table, along with pumps and empty buckets, encourage children to create and control water flow.

Guiding children's focused explorations requires the teacher to know which property of water she is helping children explore or reflect upon. Therefore the next section of the guide presents three distinct focused explorations of water that teachers can match to their children's interests. These focused explorations are named Flow, Drops, and Sink and Float. Teachers can choose to facilitate them one after another, in any order, or simultaneously.

Of course, providing children with the time and materials they need to focus on a particular property of water is just the beginning! Teachers continue to facilitate science talks, but now they focus the discussions on particular properties of water and what children are noticing as they engage in exploration that might result in evidence for their developing theories.

Rainy-day walks; visits to a water works, stream, or harbor; or a look under the sink gives children opportunities to compare their water explorations to what they see away from the water table and water center(s). Guest visitors can share their knowledge and enthusiasm for working with water. Sailors, plumbers, and people who design sprinkler systems can provide children with new information about how the properties of water influence real-world work. Books and Web sites offer still images of water, which can help children look more closely at how water moves and the shapes it takes as they engage in their own explorations. The extension section (p. 89) has suggestions for field trips, guest visitors, and books. See the section on science teaching (p. 95) for information about young children's inquiry and for strategies you can use to focus and deepen their experience and thinking during the exploration.

TEACHER NOTE: It was a rainy day so we went outside to play in the puddles. A group of four children became intrigued with the water running out of the drain pipe. It was beginning to make a stream. They busily piled sticks and stones to dam it, to see how high they could get their puddle to fill, and then they broke the dam and watched the water flood their stream. When we got back inside, we talked about how hard it was to hold back the water with the sticks and stones; how quickly the water flowed into the stream once the dam broke. Amy and Melissa asked if they could make a river outside again. If it doesn't rain soon, I'll see if I can get the custodian to hook up the hose for us.

focused exploration: flow

This focused exploration supports children as they pursue their interest in making water move. Steps 1 and 2 focus on moving water through tubing; steps 3 and 4 are about smaller streams of water flowing from holes in cups and bottles. With the introduction of new materials that encourage them to move water from one height to another, children have opportunities to explore in a more dramatic way the effects gravity, air pressure, water pressure, and their own muscle power (squeezing a baster; pushing the handle on a pump) have on how water flows and on their ability to control moving water. As children continue to incorporate new materials in their play throughout the exploration, they discuss, represent, and revisit their work, developing theories about how and why what they do makes water move in particular ways.

Step 1: Moving Water through Tubes

This step introduces children to the wire water wall, a structure placed in the water table that allows children to secure funnels and tubing in various positions. It also introduces children to connectors for attaching tubing. Children explore the materials in various combinations to move water up, down, and sideways. They also have opportunities to observe air as it passes through and gets stuck in the tubing. And because the wire water wall holds tubing and funnels in place, children confront how water level affects flow and begin to develop theories about how and why what they do makes water move in particular ways.

CORE EXPERIENCES

☐ Use a wire water wall and connected clear tubing to move water in various ways.

☐ Reflect on how water can be made to move in particular ways.

☐ Reflect on the exploration with a discussion of ways water is represented in picture books.

PREPARATION

☐ Display books and posters with images of streams, waterfalls, and connected water pipes.

☐ Put together a wire water wall. (See "Essential Information" on p. 103 of the resources section for information on setting up a wire water wall.)

☐ Check to make sure that the plastic connectors fit into the clear tubing made available during open exploration.

SCHEDULE

Set the schedule for the next week, or until all interested children have explored with the new materials.

☐ 5–10 minutes for an introductory meeting with the whole group

☐ 45–60 minutes for choice time, four or five times during the week

☐ 10–15 minutes for weekly discussions with the whole group

MATERIALS

☐ A picture book about water illustrated in simple drawings (See "Books and Web Sites" on p. 108 of the resources section for book suggestions.)

☐ Copies of the observation record form (p. 116)

At the Water Table

☐ Clear cups and containers

☐ Clear tubing

☐ Funnels

☐ Basters and squirt bottles

☐ Wire water wall (See "Essential Information" on p. 103 of the resources section.)

☐ Additional tubing (at least 18 inches in length)

☐ Y- and T-connectors that fit into your different-size tubing

☐ Two or three clothespins or other kinds of clips to hold the wire water wall together

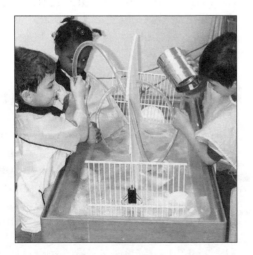

At the Water Center

☐ Clear tubs of water

☐ Clear cups and containers

☐ Clear tubing

☐ Funnels

☐ Basters and squirt bottles

☐ Wire rack for each tub (See "Essential Information" on p. 103 of the resources section for suggestions.)

☐ Y- and T-shaped connectors that fit into your different-size tubing

FAMILY CONNECTION

Send a note home to families about the children's focused exploration of moving water. Suggest they take rainy-day walks with their children to look for water running down drain pipes, gutters, roofs, and sidewalks. Some families may want to look through their collection of kitchen utensils for a baster and large plastic straws to add to their children's bath toys.

TEACHING PLAN

ENGAGE

Introduce children to the focus on water flow.

Share experiences.

Gather children together in a circle and invite them to share experiences they have had playing with flowing water. Begin the conversation by saying something such as the following:

- *When have you seen water moving?*
- *What do you think was making it move?*
- *Tell us about a time you've played with a garden hose, under a faucet, or in water running down the sidewalk on a rainy day.*

Extend the conversation by asking questions from the following list:

- *What happened to the water when it came out of the faucet, garden hose, or gutter?*
- *What did it feel like? What happened when you put your hand in the water? What happened when the water hit the grass? Sidewalk? Bottom of the sink?*
- *How were you able to make it stop? Slow down? Go faster? Go in a different direction?*
- *What about the tubes in the water table? How have you been getting water to go through them? How have you made the water go faster? Slower? Stop? Change direction? Go up?*

EXAMPLE: This is one example of how a wire rack can be used in a tub at the water center to provide children with a place to hold materials as they explore moving water up and down.

ISSUE: *I can't find the material for the wire rack. Do I need one to do these activities?*

RESPONSE: Besides referring to the resources section mentioned on p. 38, try to keep in mind that the point of the wire rack is to provide a structure to help children hold the tubing and funnels, which can free their hands to work. Any way you can find to make this possible for children is fine. You might put a cube made from large waffle blocks or a child-size chair into the tub or water table.

EXAMPLE: This photo shows how some children used a wire water wall to hold their materials.

Introduce the connectors and the wire water wall.

Show children the connectors and demonstrate how they can be used to put tubes together. Ask children to predict where the water will go once it's poured into one of the connected tubes. Tell children that during choice time they will be able to connect their own tubes and fill them with water.

Show children the wire water wall. Tell them that it will be added to the water table and invite children to share ideas about what they might do with it. Ask questions such as the following:

- *How might you use this wire wall in the water table?*

- *What do you think will happen to the water when you do that?*

- *How do you think you will use this wire wall to help you move water?*

Demonstrate how funnels can be held with clothespins to the wire wall and how tubes can be stuck through the wall's slats and held in place.

Tell children that the wire water wall will be at the water table for the next few weeks and that it can help hold their tubing and funnels.

Next, show children the wire racks that will go in tubs at the water center. Tell them that the wire racks will be in the tubs at the water center for the next few weeks and can help hold up containers and tubing.

EXPLORE

Support children's initial exploration, until all interested children have participated.

Observe and document the exploration.

Spend a few minutes observing children as they engage in water play. Use the observation record form on p. 116 to document what you notice about how children are moving and controlling water. Observe the following:

- How are they making the water move through the tubing?

- Are they controlling the water flow? If so, how are they stopping it? Slowing it down? Making it go faster? Making it change direction?

- Are they generating their own challenges? If so, what kinds of challenges are they creating for themselves?

- What kind of cooperative play are you noticing?

- What kinds of play are children engaged in?
  - Are they inventing and playing water games?
  - Are they building machines or fountains?
  - Are they pretending to be someone else, such as a plumber or a magic-potion maker?

Use your observations and notes to facilitate the upcoming science talk.

ISSUE: *If I introduce the wire water wall before children get to use it on their own, will I have a negative influence on their creative exploration by sharing my own way of doing things?*

RESPONSE: The purpose of introducing the wire water wall before children use it is to help them think of its possibilities, not as something that needs to be used correctly. Encourage children to share with one another their ideas about how the wall can be used to hold materials or as a prop in their water play.

EXAMPLE: This teacher acknowledged children's exploration by helping them thread tubing through the very top of the wire water wall.

Interact and talk with interested children, keeping the focus on the water flow.

Some children may need you to help them push connectors into tubing. Others may need help weaving their tubing through the wire water wall. By being attentive to children's needs, you acknowledge their exploration.

Another way of acknowledging children's exploration is to describe some of the ways they are using connected tubes or the wire water wall to move and control water. For example, you might say the following:

- *The water went down this tube and then, when it got to the connector, it flowed into both of these smaller tubes.*

- *The water came out really fast when you poured it through the funnel attached to the top of the wire water wall.*

- *Look! When you lifted the tubing up, the water stopped coming out of this end!*

Some children may welcome questions about their explorations. Ask a question or two and continue conversations with interested children. Help them focus on the ways they are controlling water flow by asking questions such as the following:

- *Where did the water go? What happened?*

- *How did you get the water to stop? Go faster? Change direction?*

- *What might happen if you put your thumb over the end of the tube? Hold the tube up higher? Put the end of the tube in the water? Attach another tube to this one?*

Focus children's observations on the bubbles they see by using comments and questions such as the following:

- *I see a bubble! Do you?*

- *Where did that bubble come from?*

- *Where do you think the bubble went?*

- *Can you make more bubbles?*

- *Can you make bigger or smaller bubbles?*

Encourage all children to participate.

Offer reluctant explorers a role to play at the water table. For example, you might suggest a child hold one end of a long tube while you hold the other so you can send water back and forth to one another. Another idea is to partner active water explorers with children who have not yet used the wire water wall.

EXTEND

Use books and a close look at plumbing to extend the exploration.

ISSUE: *I try to get children to talk about what they are doing by asking them open-ended questions—but they don't respond very much.*

RESPONSE: Children do not always respond verbally when they are busily engaged in water play. And as adults, we often try too hard to encourage children to respond to our questions. Don't worry if children don't talk much while they are engaged; try asking fewer questions and either observe quietly or make a few comments about what the children are doing.

TEACHER NOTE: Celia is a second language learner who loves to play at the water table area. One day she stuck a tube through the wire water wall and attached a funnel to the other end. She poured water into the funnel and stared at the other end of the tubing, hoping it would flow out, but it didn't. She tried pushing water into the full funnel with a spoon, but that didn't work. She tried using a baster to push the water up into the tube, and that didn't work either. Finally, she lifted the funnel end up and to her surprise, water started flowing out of the other end of the tube.

Celia: *The water coming!*

Teacher: *What did you do to get it to come out?*

Celia: *I did like that.*

Teacher: *You held the funnel up?*

Celia: *It fall down. More water fall down.*

Teacher: *What happens when you hold the funnel down again?*

Read aloud to the whole group.

Read a picture book with illustrations of water drops, rain, puddles, or rivers so children can begin to think about ways water can be represented on paper. *Water* by Frank Asch, for example, is full of illustrations created in watercolor, colored pencil, and acrylics that represent water in different ways.

As you read aloud, use your fingers to outline the various colors, lines, and shapes the illustrator uses to represent water. You may want to also draw examples on a whiteboard or on chart paper and create a list of ways children might represent water drops, squirting water, flowing water, dripping water, and so on. Another idea is to ask volunteers to help you find the various ways the illustrator represented water.

Look for water pipes.

With small groups, walk around your building and look at faucets and visible water pipes. For example, visit a bathroom or kitchen sink, and turn on a faucet. Ask questions such as the following:

- *Where do you think the water comes from?*
- *Where do you think it goes?*
- *Why do you say that?*
- *How do you think the faucet stops the water?*
- *What have you used at the water table that reminds you of the faucet? How did you make the water flow? Stop flowing?*

REFLECT

In small groups, reflect at the water table and the water center near the end of choice time. Meet with the whole group to reflect during a science talk.

Initiate reflective discussions during choice time.

Just before cleanup, ask the children at the water table and the water center to show you some of what they did with the materials during choice time. Help them reflect on the ways they controlled water flow by asking questions such as the following:

- *How did you get the water to move from this side of the wire wall to that side?*
- *What did you do to make it go faster? What did you do to make it stop? Go up? Go into this tube?*

Facilitate an initial science talk focused on how and why what children do makes water move in particular ways.

Bring the children together in a circle to share and reflect on the ways they move water using the wire water wall and tubing. Refer to your observation record form and notes you made during small group discussions at the water table and water center to help you frame questions that respond to children's recent water explorations. For example, you might say and ask the following:

> **TEACHER NOTE:** After we'd walked around the school to look at faucets and pipes, Antonio went to the water table and put a tube through the wire wall. Using a baster, he pumped water into one end. When the water came out the opposite end, he smiled and pointed to the classroom water fountain.

> **TEACHER NOTE:** When I visit the water table and water center and children share what they've been doing, I take notes. Then I talk with these children about my notes and ask them if they would share their discovery with the whole group during the next science talk. Some children jump at the opportunity. Others are just beginning to offer to share.

- *I noticed that you were working together to empty the water table as fast as you could. What did you do to make the water go faster?*

- *You and Max showed me the fountain you made. What did you need to do to make it go faster? Slower? Stop?*

- *What have you noticed about the bubbles in the tubes? How do you make them move? Disappear?*

- *Show us the way you moved the water. How did you make it go? Stop? Speed up? Slow down? Go up?*

- *What do you think is the best way to get water to go fast? Slow down? Go up?*

Step 2: Moving Water through Tubes More Purposefully

This step focuses children on controlling water flow more dramatically. Children are introduced to tools for moving water faster and in greater quantities: bilge and kerosene pumps. Additional tubs, buckets, or, when possible, a second water table is added to the water table area to encourage the movement of water in more elaborate ways. This step also introduces children to ways they might represent the experiences they have moving and controlling water. Without doubt, capturing water flow on paper is difficult. With this fact in mind, children are encouraged to create representational collages, drawings, sculptures, and dances to communicate some of what they noticed about using materials to control water flow.

CORE EXPERIENCES

☐ Continue to move water through tubing in various ways.

☐ Represent moving water and reflect on how it can be controlled.

☐ Extend exploration by observing running water on a rainy day or visiting with a water engineer.

PREPARATION

Every few days, arrange tubs, funnels, or tubing in and around the water table so children begin their exploration with a new setup to explore and change. (See "Essential Information" on p. 101 of the resources section about materials used for new setup ideas.)

SCHEDULE

Set schedule for as long as interest lasts:

☐ 5–10 minutes for a meeting before each choice time

☐ 45–60 minutes for choice time, four or five times a week

☐ 10–15 minutes for a discussion with the whole group, once a week

TEACHER NOTE: Even my younger children had definite ideas about how they wanted to set up the water table. They loved to create reasons to move water from one area to another.

Materials

At the Water Table

Add:

☐ One or two kerosene pumps

☐ Bilge pump

☐ A 5-gallon or larger bucket or a 7-gallon plastic mixing tub

At the Water Center

Add:

☐ Wire racks

☐ Pumps from lotion or soap bottles

For Children's Representations

☐ Collage materials: blue yarn, paper cups, clear straws, cone-shaped coffee filters

☐ Paper, fine-tip markers, blue paint

☐ Watercolors

☐ Copies of the observation record form (p. 116)

☐ Chart labeled "How We Make Water Move from One Place to Another"

Family Connection

Send a note home suggesting families look at any water pipes or hoses they might have under their kitchen sinks or connected to a toilet or washing machine. Include questions families can use to initiate conversations about their plumbing: How do you think the water gets into the toilet? How do you think the water gets in and out of the washing machine? Where does the water come from? Where does it go?

Teaching Plan

Engage

Use five to ten minutes of daily morning meetings to review prior experiences, keep momentum going, introduce the pumps, and introduce various ways of representing experiences moving water.

Introduce children to a kerosene or bilge pump.

During a meeting with the whole group, ask children to think about how they might use the pumps at the water table area. Some children may enjoy trying to explain how the pumps work. Although the concepts of vacuum and pressure are too complex for young children to grasp, they may have interesting ideas about how the pumps move water. Ask more in-depth questions such as "What makes you think that?" to encourage discussion. (See p. 103 for more information on these materials.)

These pumps can move a lot of water, especially the bilge pump. Some children pump away without keeping track of where the water is going. Plan to keep an eye on the water table while children learn to use these tools to move more water.

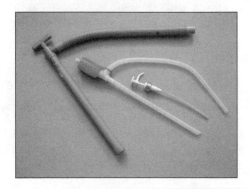

Refer to explorations from previous days.

Encourage children's continued exploration of water flow and motivate all children to participate in the exploration by focusing the group on recent events at the water table. Provide children with concrete reminders such as photographs, drawings, and materials from the water table to help them recall and share their experiences more easily. Ask questions such as the following:

- *What did you do at the water table yesterday?*
- *If your friends try it, what should they know?*
- *Here's a drawing of the way the water table area was set up yesterday. How did you get the water from here to there?*

Brainstorm new challenges.

Ask children to suggest alternative ways of setting up the water table area so they can move water in various ways from buckets to tubs and into the water table. Use chart paper to record their ideas.

Introduce children to materials and methods for representing water flow.

Show children how to use items from your art area to create collages and sculptures of the materials they are using to move and control water. Ask a child to describe or get an object they used recently to move water. Then guide the group in a discussion of their ideas for representing that object using art materials. Demonstrate their suggestions and then ask for their ideas about how they show where the water flowed into, out of, or through the object.

During another morning meeting, talk with children about drawing the materials they use to move water. Show them how to trace materials or how to use basic shapes to represent them on paper.

EXPLORE

Support children's ongoing explorations until all interested children have participated. Create renewed interest in the exploration by doing some of the following:

- Move the water table setup outdoors.
- Borrow a second water table and add it to your water area.
- Provide a child-size chair in the water table and put a bucket of water on its seat.

Continue to observe children's focused exploration of water flow.

Use the observation record forms to record what children do and say to express their developing understandings of how water can be moved and controlled. Observe the following:

- How are they becoming more intentional in the ways they move water through the tubing and control its speed and direction?
- How do they position the tubing to control water flow?
- How do they use the connectors to control the direction and amount of water flow?
- How do they move water up?

EXAMPLE: These children were eager to tell their teacher about how their juice machine worked.

EXAMPLE: Photographs can supplement teacher observational notes.

TEACHER NOTE: I heard Xavier call out, "You guys, come here! Put your hand in. See? This is getting bigger." He was sharing his strategy for measuring the changing depth of water in the bucket as it filled. I'm going to ask him to share his discovery during tomorrow's science talk.

In addition to documenting the exploration, your notes can be used to remind children of their experiences during weekly science talks.

Guide and challenge children.

You can help children focus on the ways they are creating and controlling water flow by describing what you would like them to notice. Examples of descriptive comments that focus on what children are doing to control water flowing through tubes include:

- *The water came out really fast when you held the tube up above your head.*
- *The funnel directs water into the second tube.*

Some children will initiate conversation. Use these opportunities to learn about the kinds of water play children are engaged in and the ways they are moving water. Use comments and questions such as the following:

- *I noticed that Maria used a funnel attached to a tube to fill up this skinny bottle. You filled it up in a different way. How did you fill it up?*
- *Now that you've told me how you built your fountain, will you show me how you turn it on? How do you get it to stop flowing? I wonder if you can get it to flow over here too.*
- *Where did the juice in your machine go? How do you make it go over the wire water wall? Why do you think you need the baster to get the juice over the wall?*
- *Watch what happens when Victor pours water down that tube. Is that what happened when you did it? Why do you think the water stops flowing when it gets to that point?*

When children see bubbles, ask them what they notice about how the bubbles move, their shapes and sizes, and wonder aloud about where the bubbles came from. Invite children to share their theories.

Some children welcome suggestions or challenges generated from teachers.

- Challenge children to see if they can get water to come out of both sides of the T- or Y-shaped connector at the same time.
- Challenge children to see if they can get water to come out of just one side of the T- or Y-shaped connector at one time.
- Suggest children empty one water table into another using the connected tubes.

Encourage all children to explore water flow.

Add props that might interest your reluctant water explorers. For example, office supplies such as a telephone or notebooks of plumbing supplies might interest children in using the water table area as a plumber's workshop.

Remember to have materials accessible for children who are unable to access the water table or tubs because of physical limitations.

TEACHER NOTE: Juan noticed how fast he was able to move water with the bilge pump.

> **Juan:** *This one goes faster.*
>
> **Teacher:** *What goes faster?*
>
> **Juan:** *The water . . . it moves faster into the cups. It spills them and makes them fall. This [bilge pump] is bigger than that [kerosene pump]. It goes harder and faster.*
>
> **Teacher:** *Do they both do the same job?*
>
> **Juan:** *They can make the water go where you point it*

EXAMPLE: These three- and four-year-olds were determined to empty all of the water in one table into another one. They decided they had to move all the water through tubing.

Some children may have an aversion to getting wet. They may feel most comfortable engaging in water play when they can use materials that allow them to move water without getting wet—for example, basters and squirt bottles.

Have children record or represent their experiences.

Introduce children to various ways they can record aspects of their exploration. Examples include the following:

- Use a measuring stick to find out how high children can move water up a tube or how far they can move water across the classroom. Record these lengths on chart paper.

- Count out loud to find out how long children can keep their fountain flowing or how many glasses of juice their machine can fill in a minute. Introduce the concept of making tally marks to record numbers.

As you visit the water table and the water center, invite children to represent what they notice about moving water. You might choose from the following:

- Ask children to use their fingers to show the path the water took as they moved it.

- Sketch the materials children are using on a whiteboard or chart paper and then invite them to use a blue marker to draw the path they made the water take.

- Offer collage materials for children to use to represent the water materials they've been using and then ask them to add blue string, ribbon, or marker to represent where they made the water go.

Create a documentation panel.

Use your sketches or photographs along with children's work to create a documentation panel that illustrates children's strategies for moving and controlling water. Include the words children use to explain how and why what they do makes water move in particular ways. (See "Guidelines for Creating Documentation Panels" on p. 115 for guidance.) You can use this panel for upcoming science talks and to share with families and colleagues.

EXTEND

Invite a guest expert into the classroom to help extend children's water exploration. Explore water flow outdoors in the rain.

Invite a plumber or water engineer to visit with the children.

Introduce children to a dramatic role they can play while they use clear tubing to explore water flow. For example, invite a plumber into the classroom. Ask the visiting plumber to talk about what he does, and invite him to share designs, tools, books, and stories related to his work. (See the extension activities on p. 91 for more information about extending children's inquiry with guest experts.)

ISSUE: *My children are too involved with what they are doing to focus on representation.*

RESPONSE: Helping children reflect on how the streams move and change is what is important here. Drawing is one way to encourage closer observation and reflection. But there are other ways too. Some children will use their hands and bodies; others will use words.

TEACHER NOTE: During one of our science talks, we discussed what works best for making water move up tubes. I used children's words and drawings along with my own photographs and drawings to make this documentation panel. We referred to it quite often throughout the exploration.

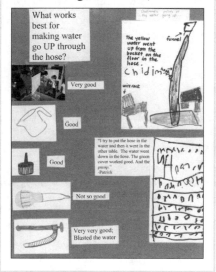

EXAMPLE: This visiting plumber shared pieces of PVC pipe and compared it with tubing and connectors.

Allow children time to ask questions. Encourage them to share photos or use demonstration to show the visiting plumber how they have been moving and controlling water.

Explore water flow outdoors on a rainy day.

Help children notice flowing water outdoors. On rainy days, invite small groups to look out the window at rain flowing through downspouts, sloping roofs, sidewalks, or their playground slide.

If the rainfall is light and without thunder or lightning, bring a group of children together and tell them that they will be going on a rainy-day walk to look at moving water. Help them focus on the task by asking questions such as the following: "Where do you think we will see the fastest-moving water? Why do you say that?"

Once outdoors, guide children towards gutters, slides, sloped sidewalks, and other nearby surfaces that are funneling moving water. Ask the children to think of ways they might stop the flowing water. If possible, allow them to test their ideas.

Back indoors, over lunch or at the next group meeting, ask children to help you list the places they saw moving water outdoors. Some children may want to help you identify the places where the water was moving the fastest.

If children were able to try stopping some of the flowing rain water, invite them to share their strategies. Ask children if their ideas worked—or did not work—and why some of their ideas may have worked better than others.

REFLECT

Reflect at the water table and the water center in small groups near the end of choice time. Gather the whole group to reflect during weekly science talks.

Conduct discussions with small groups during choice time.

Before the end of choice time, meet with children who have been using the water table area. Ask them to tell you what they did, noticed, or discovered that day. In the context of their play, help children reflect on the ways they made water move and why those ways worked by asking questions such as the following:

- *How did you get the juice from here to there?*

- *How did you turn the car wash on and off? Why do you think that works?*

- *When did the potion move the fastest? How do you think you got it to move that fast?*

- *How do you think the water got up over the chair?*

Some children may want to continue the discussion by making a representational collage or drawing of how they moved water through tubing.

TEACHER NOTE: The big point I wanted the children to come away from our river visit with was that water flow can change direction, especially when something gets in its way. I asked the children what they noticed about what the water was doing and I wrote down their comments so we could reflect on them back in the classroom.

Desirice: *It goes around the rocks.*

Terrance: *It kinda goes underneath where the big waves are.*

EXAMPLE: Autumn said, "I made a water table with a wall. The water was dripping down and a bubble kept coming up. The water landed on the pillow!" As part of their conversation, the teacher asked these questions: "Where were the drips coming from? Where did they go? Where were the bubbles coming from? Where did they go?"

I made a watertable with a wall. The water was dripping down and a bubble kept coming up.

The water landed on the pillow!

May 2001 by Autumn

Conduct weekly science talks with the whole group.

Once a week, bring your whole group together in a circle to discuss their strategies for moving and controlling water in clear tubing and how the water moved. Encourage them to think about why their strategies work as well. Record children's ideas on the chart labeled "How We Make Water Move from One Place to Another."

Begin by offering concrete props for children to use in describing ways they have been moving water through tubing. Examples include the following:

- Representational drawing, painting, or collage
- Photograph
- Documentation panel
- Materials from the water table

Help children describe their experiences by asking questions such as the following:

- *Where did the water go?*
- *Was it going fast? Slow? Did it ever stop? Did it go up? How?*

Then help children reflect on how and why they are able to move and control water. Use questions such as the following:

- *How do you get water to go up a tube? Why do you think that works? What other ways might you get water up the tube? Why do you think that would work? When does water flow up? Down? Why do you think that is?*
- *How do you get water to flow faster and faster? Slow down? Stop? Go in two directions? Why do you think that works?*

Step 3: Water in Bottles with Holes

Gravity pulls all things down, including water. Air and water pressure also affect water flow. Bottles with holes in their bottoms or sides, when used in water play, highlight the effects these forces have on water flow. As children use these bottles that have holes of different sizes in their bottoms, you can help them notice the difference in the sizes and behavior of the water as it streams out. As children make and control streams of water using bottles with holes down the sides, you can help them notice how the streams change as the bottle or cup empties. Find time to play with these bottles again yourself. Notice how the amount of water in a bottle and the size of the holes affect the kinds of streams created.

ISSUE: *What's the point of making and posting charts of children's ideas when they cannot read them?*

RESPONSE: Charts are worth your time and effort when they are meaningful and useful. They can be meaningful when children see them as records that they can refer to as their ideas change or new information is discovered. That's why it's important to record the name of each child next to his idea, and it helps to draw a sketch of the idea as a cue as well. It's also important to refer back to charts as the exploration continues, to remind children of their earlier ideas. Use charts as working documents, crossing out and rewriting children's ideas as they change.

TEACHER NOTE: I brought a funnel attached to tubing to the science talk. I held it in the shape of a U and asked children to think about what might happen if we were to pour water into it.

Kassandra: *It would go down to here and stop, right . . . here.*

Jeff: *If you hold it like this (with the funnel lower than the other end of the tube), it will go down and shoot out of the end!*

Evelyn: *If you hold it like this (in a perfect U shape), it just gets caught.*

I invited the children to test their predictions. After each test I asked, "How do you think the water did that?"

Kassandra: *The funnel can't push it all that way.*

Jeff: *It's really a fountain.*

Evelyn: *It needs to be squirted with the baster.*

CORE EXPERIENCES

☐ Explore streams made using bottles with holes in their bottoms and bottles with holes in their sides.

☐ Notice changes in size and direction of the flow of the streams.

☐ Begin to reflect on what causes streams to change.

PREPARATION

Display posters and books with clear, large images of fountains, showers, or sprinklers around the classroom.

SCHEDULE

Set the schedule for several weeks, allowing enough time for all children to have initial experiences exploring bottles with holes.

☐ 5–10 minutes for an introductory meeting with the whole group

☐ 45–60 minutes for choice time, four or five times during the week

☐ 10–15 minutes for weekly discussions with the whole group

MATERIALS

At Both the Water Table and the Water Center(s)

☐ Cups without holes for pouring water into bottles with holes

☐ three or four clipboards with paper and markers

☐ four or more bottles with holes in their bottoms

☐ four or more bottles with holes down their sides

(See "Essential Information" on p. 103 of the resources section for detailed descriptions of how to make these bottles.)

FAMILY CONNECTION

Send a note home telling families about children's exploration of streams using bottles with holes. Use a sketch to explain how they can cut the tops off water bottles, and poke two or three holes in them so they can add bottles with holes to their children's bath toys. Include possible questions for adults to ask as they facilitate conversations about streams with children who are playing with bottles with holes: "What will happen if you put your finger over one of the holes? How can we make the streams get smaller? Go further? Get bigger?"

TEACHING PLAN

ENGAGE

Introduce bottles with holes in a meeting with the whole group for five to ten minutes.

Children's interest in using these materials to move water may last for quite awhile. If interest is high, keep going! If you have two water tables, you can keep the wire water wall in one and use the second as you proceed to step 3: "Water in Bottles with Holes."

TEACHER NOTE: The four children at the water center told me what they noticed about making streams.

Nate: *Mine dribbled from the top hole. And it sorta dribbled from the middle hole. But it squirted out of the bottom hole.*

Julia: *Mine squirted out of all the holes at once.*

Connor: *Only if you put it all the way to the very top. Then it squirts out all of the holes.*

Katherine: *The water came out of the bottom two holes the most on mine.*

Then I requested that they all fill their bottles up to the top and see what happens to their streams as the water empties.

Connor: *See, that's what I mean. They squirt out at first but then they turn into dribbles.*

Introduce bottles with holes.

During a meeting with the whole group before choice time, show the children a bottle with a hole in its bottom. Ask: "What do you think you will see when we fill this bottle with water? How do you think it will change as we watch it?"

After you've filled the bottle and the group has watched the stream, ask the following:

- *What did you see happen? How did the stream change?*

- *What do you think will happen if I put my finger over the hole and then fill the bottle with water again? Why do you say that?*

Again, pour water into the bottle, but this time keep your finger over the hole. Ask: "What happened? Why do you think that happened?" Next, show the children a bottle with holes down its side. Ask: "What do you think you will see when the bottle is filled with water? How will the streams change?"

After you've poured water into the bottle, process the experience with questions such as the following:

- *What happened?*

- *What do you think will happen if I put my finger over one of the holes and then fill the bottle with water again? Why do you say that?*

Again, pour water into the bottle, but this time keep your finger over a hole. Ask: "What happened? Why do you think that happened?" Tell children that there are bottles of different sizes with holes at the water table and in a tub at the water center. As you transition to choice time, remind children on their way to the water table and water center about looking for how the streams change.

EXPLORE

Support and encourage children as they explore streams.

Observe children's initial exploration of streaming water.

Sit with children as they explore bottles with holes. Use an observation form to take notes about what the children are noticing and doing. Observe the following:

- Do they notice the different-size streams coming out? Are they making a connection between the size of the hole and the way the stream looks?

- What do they notice about streams as they change? Size? How long they last? When they start to drip?

- Do they try to control the streams? How?

Make sketches or take photos to supplement your observational notes.

TEACHER NOTE: Maija was fascinated by the way the stream looked "like a twirly slide."

I asked her why she thought it looked like that and she said, "The hole's funny."

I probed her thinking with another question: "What do you mean by 'funny'?"

Maija pointed to the unevenness of the hole caused by the pen she'd used to make the holes, and I asked, "What do you think will happen if we make that hole nice and round? Show me!"

Encourage children to focus on the streams.

Focus children's attention on some of what you would like them to notice about the streams by describing changes in the streams. You might say something such as the following:

- *Look! That stream is starting to drip! I wonder why that happened.*

- *This stream was shooting straight out, and now it's squirting down. The same thing is happening to Irene's bottle.*

Talk with children about what they are noticing. Ask questions such as the following:

- *What's happening to that stream?*

- *Are all the streams the same? Why do you think that is?*

- *What do you think will happen if you fill the bottle up to the top with water?*

Introduce drawing as a way to represent water streaming from bottles with holes.

As you visit the water table and water center, use a clipboard, paper, and marker to sketch one of the bottles with holes that children are using. Invite children to add lines to show streams they see coming from the bottle. The streams will change, but you can encourage children to draw what they see happening at any one point. Some children may choose to draw the bottles with the holes themselves, as well as the streams. Offer these children a clipboard, marker, and a piece of blank paper. Ask children what they notice about the streams they drew, or how they changed, and write their words next to their drawings.

REFLECT

Reflect at the water table and the water center in small groups near the end of choice time. Gather the whole group to reflect during weekly science talks.

Conduct small group discussions during choice time.

Toward the end of choice time, meet with the children at the water table or at the water center. Ask them to show you how they made streams and some of the things they noticed about the sizes and shapes of the streams.

Encourage descriptive language and analytical thinking with questions such as the following:

- *How did you make the stream? What did it look like?*

- *How did the stream change? What do you think made them change?*

- *Which holes make the best streams? Why do you say that?*

- *When you put water in this bottle, what did the streams look like? How did they change? Can you show me?*

- *What did you do to make this stream reach this other cup? Can you show me?*

- *What do you think makes streams go far? Why do you think that is?*

EXAMPLE: These drawings were done by children who were exploring streams in bottles with holes on their sides. The teacher recorded their answers to the question "What happened?" and then used the drawings to talk with the children about why they thought the streams changed as the water level in the bottles got lower.

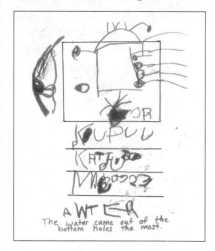

The water came out of the bottom holes the most.

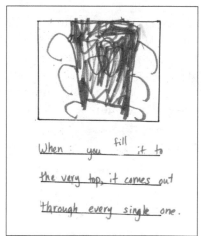

When you fill it to the very top, it comes out through every single one.

Conduct a science talk with the whole group.

Gather the whole group together in a circle to talk about the streams they have been making and focus on the difference in streams and how they change. Use photographs or drawings from the exploration, or bring actual bottles with holes to focus the science talk.

- *What happened when you used the bottles with holes in their bottoms?*
  - *Did all of their streams look the same? Why do you think that is?*
  - *Why do you think some of the streams turned into drips earlier than others did?*
- *What happened when you used the bottles with holes down their sides?*
  - *How did you get the water to squirt out far?*
  - *Which streams squirt the farthest? Why do you think that is?*
  - *What happens when the water runs out? How do the streams change? Why do you think that is?*

Step 4: Water in Bottles with Holes Continues

The more opportunities children have to play with bottles with holes, record their observations, and reflect on their experiences creating and manipulating streams, the more they will notice and the more they will have to think about. With the addition of a Velcro pegboard to hold bottles with holes in various positions, children can look more closely at the ways streams change size, shape, and direction in relationship to the amount of water each bottle contains and the placement and size of its holes.

CORE EXPERIENCES

- ☐ Use a Velcro pegboard to think about and arrange bottles with holes.
- ☐ Focus on how the placement and size of holes in bottles, as well as the amount of water in each, affect changes in streams.

PREPARATION

- ☐ Position either the water table or a large tub near a wall (or some other stable backdrop) so the top of the pegboard can lean and be secured against the wall and the bottom of it can sit inside the water table or tub.
- ☐ Identify sprinklers or fountains in the neighborhood for children to visit and observe.
- ☐ Search the Internet for images of sprinklers and fountains to print, enlarge, and show to children (see the resources section on p. 110 for suggestions of sites).

ISSUE: *The children are sharing what they do but they don't have much to say when I ask them to explain what is happening or why they think so.*

RESPONSE: Encourage children's responses, but don't push them. Props, sketches, and photographs can give them something to refer to and makes communicating ideas easier. As they continue their explorations, help them look more closely and encourage small groups to notice what happens when water runs out of the bottles.

SCHEDULE

☐ 5–10 minutes for a meeting before each choice time

☐ 45–60 minutes for choice time, four or five times a week

☐ 10–15 minutes for a discussion with the whole group, once a week

MATERIALS

☐ Pipe cleaners or pieces of craft wire (six or more), about a dozen Styrofoam cups, a whiteboard or chart paper for children to use to represent their bottles and streams

☐ Copies of the observation record form (p. 116)

☐ Chart labeled: "Our Ideas about Bottles with Holes"

At the Water Table

☐ Clear plastic cups without holes

☐ Clipboards, paper, and markers

☐ A Velcro pegboard and Velcro bottles with holes as described in "Essential Information" on p. 103 of the resources section

☐ Clear plastic funnels

At the Water Center

☐ Clear tubs of water

☐ Cups without holes

☐ Wire racks

☐ Bottles with holes

☐ Clipboards, paper, and markers

☐ Styrofoam cups, pencils, several fat nails (such as roofing nails)

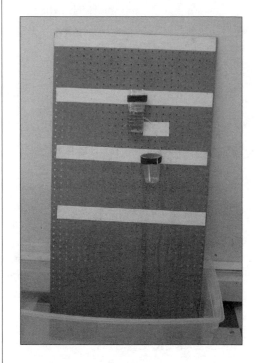

FAMILY CONNECTION

Invite families to play with the Velcro pegboard when they come to pick their children up. Or plan a "Water Play Open House" one afternoon or evening so children can show their families what they do with the Velcro pegboard and the wire water wall.

TEACHING PLAN

ENGAGE

Introduce the Velcro pegboard and how to make cups with holes. Review what they are finding out, and keep children's momentum going by engaging them in exploring streams of water.

Introduce the Velcro pegboard in a meeting with the whole group.

Bring a tub of water and some bottles with holes to the whole group meeting.

Refer to children's exploration of streams by describing some of what you have heard and observed at the water table recently. For example, you might say something such as the following:

- *Several of you have noticed that streams change as a bottle runs out of water. Let's watch what happens when I fill these two bottles with water. What do you see happening?*

Tell the children that you want to show them something that will help hold the bottles with holes so they can look more carefully at what happens to the streams as the bottles run out of water.

Introduce the group to the Velcro pegboard and a few Velcro bottles with holes. Show them how the bottles stick to the pegboard and how the bottles can be twisted and moved. Tell the children that the pegboard will either sit in a tub or the water table, leaning against a wall. Finally, show children how to use a pencil to make a few holes in a Styrofoam cup and tell them that cups and pencils will be added to the water center so children who want to make their own cups with holes can go there.

EXPLORE

Support and encourage children as they explore streams.

Continue to observe children's focused exploration of streams.

Use an observation form, sketches, and, if possible, a camera to document what you notice about how children are making and controlling streams. Observe and record the following:

- Do they intentionally move bottles in order to make their streams go where they want?
- Do they see a relationship between the amount of water in the bottles and the ways the streams change? For example, do they try to keep their bottles full if they want their streams to squirt out as far as possible?
- How do they stop streams?

Focus and challenge children as they explore streams.

Focus children's attention on interesting phenomena by describing some of your observations. For example, you might say the following:

- *That stream is getting smaller and smaller.*
- *Every time you pour more water into the bottle, the streams change.*

Some children welcome teacher input. For children who are using bottles with holes in the bottom, focus their observations and thinking on the effect the size of the hole has on the stream by suggesting something such as the following:

- Fill two bottles with holes in their bottoms with water; make sure one has a small hole and the other has a large hole. Hold them next to each other. What's different about them? Why do you think that is?

ISSUE: *My children just pour water into the bottles and don't bother to move the bottles around.*

RESPONSE: That's fine. They are exploring the relationship between the amount of water they add to the bottles and what happens to the streams. If you want to encourage them to see what happens when they arrange the bottles in groups, you can always suggest they make one bottle stream into another, and then into a third bottle.

EXAMPLE: Julia created a challenge for herself by trying to get all of the streams going at the same time. She discovered the importance of filling the cup up as much as possible.

For children who are using bottles with holes in their sides, focus their observations and thinking on the effect the amount of water in a bottle has on its streams by suggesting something such as the following:

- Fill a bottle with holes in its sides and watch what happens as water streams out. Does the same thing happen when you fill other bottles with holes in their sides? Why do you think that is?

Encourage children to make their own cups by poking their own cups with short, fat nails. Suggest they try some very little holes, some fat holes, some on the bottom, and others on the side. Try making your own cups with holes too. Notice how the size of a hole affects its stream.

If possible, take photos of these comparisons so children can refer back to them when they share their observations and thinking with the whole group during an upcoming science talk.

Create a documentation panel.

Use your sketches, photographs, children's representations, and excerpts from their conversations to create a documentation panel that shows what children are noticing and thinking about one of the following:

- How and why streams change as bottles empty
- How and why the size of the hole in the bottom of a bottle affects the way its stream changes

Cover the panel with plastic and hang it near the water table so children can refer to it as they play. You will also use the panel during upcoming science talks, and you can always share it with families and colleagues.

EXTEND

Use books and the outdoors to extend the exploration.

Share photos of fountains.

During morning meeting share photos (8 by 10 inches or larger) of sprinklers and fountains with the group. Ask them if they have seen fountains or sprinklers, and to tell how they are alike or different from the ones in the photos.

Hold up one of the photos and ask children to compare the streams in one of the photos to the streams they make with bottles with holes. Ask: "What makes the streams in this fountain or sprinkler? Why do you say that?"

Play in sprinklers or with garden hoses.

If the weather permits, encourage children to play outdoors with a sprinkler or hose to make streams of water move in various ways. Suggest they point the streams in different directions to see what happens. If possible, take photos of their outdoor exploration of streams and use them during an upcoming meeting as you ask the following:

TEACHER NOTE: Elizabeth told me that the top holes always made dribbles and not streams. I asked her why she thought that happened. She said, "It's because the holes are too small." I gave her a pencil to make the holes bigger, and we filled them with water again.

EXAMPLE: One teacher poked holes in plastic buckets and encouraged children to explore streams on a bigger scale, outdoors. The children pretended they were making their own fountains.

- *How is the sprinkler like the bottles with holes on their sides? How is it different?*

- *How is the hose like a bottle that has just one hole in the bottom?*

REFLECT

Reflect at the water table and the water center in small groups near the end of choice time. Gather the whole group to reflect during weekly science talks.

Conduct discussions with small groups during choice time.

During choice time, meet with children who have been using bottles and cups with holes. Invite them to show you some of the things they did with the bottles and cups, and what they noticed about the streams they made.

Use questions and comments such as the following to help children reflect on their observations and ideas about streams:

- *What happened when you made a cup with teeny holes? One big hole?*

- *How did you get the streams to squirt out far? Why do you think that works?*

- *Do all of the bottles with holes in the bottom make the same kind of stream? Why do you think that is?*

- *Do all of the bottles with holes down their sides make the same kinds of streams? Why do you think that is?*

Conduct weekly science talks with the whole group.

Once a week, bring your whole group together in a circle. As children share their experiences with the group or they discuss a documentation panel, help them reflect on the ways their streams change depending on the following:

- The amount of water in the bottle

- Where the holes were located

- The size of the hole(s)

Help the children analyze ways they have learned to control the streams by asking questions such as the ones that follow, and recording their ideas in words and sketches on the chart labeled "Our Ideas about Bottles with Holes."

- *What does the stream coming out of the bottom of a bottle with one hole in it look like? How does it change? Why do you think that happens?*

- *What are the best ways to get a stream to shoot out of the sides of a bottle really far? To stop? To dribble? Why do you think that works?*

- *What do you have to do to keep the stream from turning into a dribble? Why do you think that works?*

- *What might happen if you put your finger over one of the holes and then poured more water in the bottle? Why do you think that happens?*

TEACHER NOTE: Silvia noticed that the sprinkler made streams that never turned into dribbles.

I asked, "Why do you think that happens?"

She replied, "Because there's always water coming."

When it was time to leave and we turned the faucet off, she watched the sprinkler's streams get smaller and smaller, and when they finally turned into dribbles, she said, "Hmmm. It ran out of water."

EXAMPLE:

OUR IDEAS ABOUT BOTTLES WITH HOLES

HUGH: Big holes make big streams.

NINA: More water makes them shoot out the sides.

CELIA: Too many holes isn't good; it goes out too fast.

MIKE: The top ones don't work.

ROSE: Use a big bottle and big holes if you want big streams.

Encourage children who have been making and using their own cups with holes to share their cups and their thinking as well. Ask the following:

- *What kinds of holes did you make?*
- *What happens to the streams when the cups aren't full?*
- *What kinds of streams do the big holes make? The small holes? Why do you think that happens?*

focused exploration: drops

Drops are small "pieces" of water and typically go unnoticed by children when they are engaged in water play at the water table. Looking closely at drops and how their shapes and movements change from one surface to another provides children fundamental experience with two important properties of water: it sticks to itself (cohesion), and it sticks more or less strongly to other things (adhesion).

This focused exploration of drops moves children's water play away from the water table and provides them opportunities to make many drops by shaking their wet hands, using eyedroppers, and controlling the flow of a faucet. They use hand lenses to look closely at drops at rest on different surfaces, and they develop theories about why some of these drops are flatter than others, and why some surfaces absorb drops and others do not. Children are also encouraged to move drops on materials and notice the various ways drops combine, separate, and travel on different surfaces. Again, they are encouraged to develop, compare, and defend theories that might explain their observations.

The addition of images from books of drops caught in motion help children look with even more insight and become critical observers of drops.

The focused exploration of drops takes place at the water center but not at the water table. The water table can be used for children's ongoing exploration of flow or streams while the exploration of drops takes place. You may also choose to keep the water table and center as they are and open a second water center for the study of drops.

Step 1: Make and Observe Drops

Water forms drops. By placing eyedroppers, hand lenses, and cups of water at the water center, away from the water table, you give children opportunities to explore an important property of water—that it sticks to itself. (See "Preparing Yourself—Science" on p. 16 of "Getting Ready.")

CORE EXPERIENCES

- ☐ Use eyedroppers to make drops.
- ☐ Use hand lenses to look more closely at drops.
- ☐ Look at photographs of drops.
- ☐ Draw drops.

PREPARATION

- ☐ Display books and photos of drops around the classroom.
- ☐ Bring a cup of blue- (or another color) tinted water and an eyedropper to the whole group meeting.
- ☐ Plan to keep the water table open for children's continued exploration of flow or streams.

SCHEDULE

- ☐ 5–10 minutes for an introductory meeting with the whole group
- ☐ 45–60 minutes for choice time, four or five times each week
- ☐ 10–15 minutes for weekly science talks

MATERIALS

- ☐ Food coloring
- ☐ Copies of the observation record form (p. 116)
- ☐ Chart labeled "What We Notice about Drops"
- ☐ Clipboards, paper, fine-line markers for children to use to make drawings of drops
- ☐ Black plastic garbage bag
- ☐ Overhead projector (optional)

At the Water Table

While children explore drops at the water center, they can focus on flow or streams at the water table and at a second water center, if possible.

At the Water Center

- ☐ Rigid plastic plates (four or more)
- ☐ Plastic eyedroppers (four or more)
- ☐ Hand lenses (four or more)
- ☐ Paper towels or a sponge for spills
- ☐ Shallow bowls of blue-tinted water (two or more)

FAMILY CONNECTION

Send a note home telling families about their children's exploration of drops. Suggest they borrow an eyedropper and hand lens over a weekend so their children can share some of what they have been doing in class. Also, suggest adults talk with children about raindrops they see on windows, jackets, blades of grass, and so on. Include questions such as the following to help adults facilitate these conversations: "What shape are these drops? How are they different? The same? What makes them move? How do they move?"

TEACHING PLAN

ENGAGE

Introduce children to the focus on drops.

Share prior experiences.

Gather your children together in a circle and invite them to share experiences they have had making or watching drops. Use questions such as the following to stimulate conversation:

- *How would you describe what a drop is?*
- *Where have you seen drops?*
- *Where did they come from?*
- *When have you felt water drops? What did they feel like? What happened to the drops?*

Show children the bowl of tinted water you brought to the meeting and invite someone to make drops on an overhead projector or a black plastic bag. Ask if another child has a different way to make drops.

Describe the different ways these children made drops. For example, you might say: "Olivia made drops with her finger and Joel made them by shaking his hand over the plastic bag." Ask questions such as the following:

- *We made drops by shaking our hands. How else might we make them?*
- *Has anyone seen drops move? Where? What did the drops do?*
- *Who can make these drops move?*

Describe the different ways children make the drops move. For example, you might say: "Miguel made the drops move by blowing on them, and Christine made them move by picking up the end of the plastic."

Introduce children to eyedroppers.

Show children the eyedroppers. Ask questions such as the following:

- *Have you seen something like this before? Where? What was it used for?*
- *What do you think this is for? Why do you say that?*

Place a few drops on an overhead projector or on a plastic plate as a way of demonstrating how to use the dropper.

Show children how to use a hand lens to look more closely at drops.

Show children a hand lens. Ask questions such as the following:

- *What do you think this is?*
- *Have you used one before? What does it do?*

Tell the group that they will be using these tools called hand lenses to look more closely at drops.

Review routines for making and looking at drops during upcoming choice times.

Before sending children off to choice time, discuss any rules or routines they will need to know before they begin exploring drops. For example, you might want to develop the following guidelines:

- Eyedroppers are for making drops on plastic plates.
- Use a sponge or paper towel to dry off a plate when they are finished exploring at the water center so their friends will have a dry place to work.

EXPLORE

Support the exploration of drops, until all children have participated.

Observe and document children's exploration of drops.

As you observe, notice which children seem to be able to work the eyedroppers. Children may struggle a bit on their own for a little while, but later in the study, exploration of drops will be enhanced by children's mastery of these skills. If a child is frustrated, ask another child to help, or help yourself.

In addition, use an observation form to record the behaviors and comments of children that indicate what they are noticing about water drops. Observe and record the following:

- What are children noticing about the drops on the plates? How they move? Combine with one another? Can be dragged around with the end of the eyedropper?
- What are children noticing about how they can use eyedroppers to make big and little drops?
- Are children noticing bubbles? Where? In the droppers? On the plate? What do they say about them?

> If this will be your children's first experience with hand lenses, provide a few small pictures from magazines for children to practice viewing before they use the lenses to look more closely at drops.

Talk with children about the drops they are making.

Reinforce the persistence children show as they learn to use eyedroppers and hand lenses by making comments such as the following:

- *You are really sticking with this! Look at the beautiful drop you just made!*
- *I noticed earlier how many times you tried to get water into the dropper, and now you did it!*

Some children will welcome comments such as the following:

- *Tell me what you are noticing.*
- *Tell me what you see when you look at the drop with the hand lens.*

Other children may welcome your questions. If so, ask questions that focus them on the nature of drops. For example, you might ask the following:

- *How long can you make the drop stay stuck to the eyedropper?*
- *What shape is the drop when it lets go of the eyedropper?*
- *What happens to the drop when you hold the dropper up high and then make the drop?*
- *What's the smallest drop you can make?*
- *What's the biggest drop you can make?*
- *What happens when you tip the plate? Turn it upside down?*

Encourage all children to explore drops.

Invite children who haven't shown interest in drops to explore with you. If needed, adapt the exploration so all children can participate. Some children may need you to make drops for them. In these cases, invite them to tell you how to make "their" drops. Ask questions such as the following:

- *How big do we want this drop to be? What should I do to make it that big?*
- *Where do we want this drop to fall?*
- *How can we make this drop move on the plate?*

Encourage children to make observational drawings of drops.

Suggest children squat down to look at drops from the side so they can notice the different shapes, heights, and widths. Provide children with clipboards, paper, and fine-tip markers so they can draw side views of their drops.

Record the words children use to describe their drops and post them on classroom walls or save them for a documentation panel.

TEACHER NOTE: In order to entice more children to the water center, I put out some pennies and challenged them to make as many drops on a single coin as they could. I also put out paper so they could record their predictions and their results.

TEACHER NOTE: I wondered aloud how I was going to draw the drops coming out of Katherine's dropper.

Katherine: *Do you know what an oval is?*

Teacher: *Yes.*

Katherine: *Well, draw a spike and then an oval under it.*

Teacher: *Is the spike on the top or the bottom?*

Katherine: *It's on the top. The drop is falling.*

Extend

Use photographs and rainy days to look more carefully at drops.

Look at photographs of drops.

Use your own photographs or ones from books or Web sites as stimuli for conversations with small groups of children. Help them compare the drops in the photographs to the ones they have been observing by asking questions such as the following: "How does this drop look like ones you make? How is it different? Why do you think that is?"

Observe drops all around.

On rainy days, for example, invite a few children at a time to look out windows that have drops on them. Help children compare the ways the drops look and are moving to what they have been noticing about the drops they have been making by asking questions such as the following:

- *How are these drops different from the ones you have been making?*

- *What do you notice about the way these drops move?*

Do the same whenever drops appear: on a pitcher of cold water, at the sink, on the grass, and so on.

Reflect

Reflect at the water center in small groups near the end of choice time. Gather the whole group to reflect during weekly science talks.

Conduct science talks with the whole group.

Each week, bring the whole group together in a circle and focus the science talk on what children have noticed about the size and shape of the drops—how drops are related and the ways they move, stay together, and break apart.

Use photographs of the drops children have been making, your sketches, and children's drawings to focus the discussion. Record their ideas on the chart labeled: "What We Notice about Drops."

If no one mentions the shape of drops, ask questions such as the following:

- *What different shapes did you see?*

- *What different sizes did you see? Why do you think drops are all round?*

- *What do you have to do to make a flat drop? A round one? Why do you think that is?*

- *What did the sides of the drops look like when you looked at them through the hand lenses?*

If no one mentions the way drops move, ask questions such as the following:

- *Tell us if anything happened to your drops when they were on the plate.*
- *What happened when two drops touched? Why do you think that happened?*
- *I noticed Sebastian tipped his plate and he said, "Look! They're sliding!" Did that happen to anyone else? What do you think makes them slide like that?*
- *I saw Charlotte dragging her eyedropper through one of her drops. Did anyone else do that? What happened?*

Step 2: Make and Observe Drops on Various Surfaces

Water sticks to itself. It also sticks to other things. In this step, children have opportunities to make drops on various surfaces and notice how the shapes and behaviors of these drops vary, depending on the surface's characteristics. With opportunities to represent and reflect on their observations, children are encouraged to develop theories about why drops look and move differently on different surfaces.

CORE EXPERIENCES

☐ Make drops on various surfaces.

☐ Represent how drops look on various surfaces.

☐ Reflect on how drops look and move differently on various surfaces and theorize about why.

PREPARATION

Plan to keep the water table open for children's continued exploration of flow or boats.

SCHEDULE

☐ 5–10 minutes for a meeting before each choice time

☐ 45–60 minutes for choice time, four or five times a week

☐ 10–15 minutes for a discussion with the whole group, once a week

MATERIALS

☐ Copies of the observation record form (p. 116)

☐ Chart: "How Drops Move on Different Materials"

TEACHER NOTE: We were talking about drops and Lenny wanted to tell us how his moved when he jiggled his plate. He was having a hard time finding the words so he just got up and wiggled. We all laughed and then I invited others to show how their drops moved. We decided that the bigger drops jiggled more than the smaller, rounder ones.

TEACHER NOTE: My three-year-olds have been fascinated by the bubbles they see. Even when they were exploring drops on different surfaces, they stopped to watch what happened to the bubbles in their eyedroppers. When I asked them where they thought the bubbles came from, Megan said, "The dropper sucked them up."

I asked her to show me what she meant. She put her eyedropper in a puddle of water sitting on a piece of aluminum foil and squeezed it. When she held the dropper up again, it was full of bubbles. I said, "Let's see if that's what's happening in Spencer's dropper."

We spent a few minutes going around the table asking each of the other three children about the bubbles in their droppers.

At the Water Center

- ☐ Rigid plastic plates

- ☐ Plastic eyedroppers

- ☐ Hand lenses

- ☐ Paper towels or a sponge

- ☐ Shallow bowls of water

- ☐ Waxed paper

- ☐ Aluminum foil

- ☐ Paper towel

- ☐ Plastic wrap

- ☐ Fabric

- ☐ Clipboards, paper, fine-line markers, glue for children to use to represent their observations

FAMILY CONNECTION

Send a note home telling families about children's exploration of drops on different surfaces. Suggest they invite their children to make drops by shaking their wet hands on objects such as the following, which they can find around the house: a plastic bag, a paper towel, an umbrella, a piece of paper with a big shape drawn in crayon, or a window pane. Include questions such as the following, which adults might use to facilitate conversations about the ways drops behave on different surfaces: "What shapes are these drops? How are they moving? Where are they going? How do they look like other drops you've made or seen? How do they look different?"

TEACHING PLAN

ENGAGE

Introduce new materials during a meeting with the whole group.

Introduce children to new materials.

During a whole group meeting before choice time, invite children to share what they have noticed about the shape of drops. You might say the following: "You've been making and looking at drops. What shapes are your drops making?" Some children may want to show shapes with their hands or their bodies, and others may want to use a whiteboard or chart paper to draw their shape.

Next, ask children to share what they have noticed about the movement of the drops by asking: "How do your drops move on the plates?"

Invite children to use their hands or bodies to mimic the movement of the drops they've been making.

Then show children a 6 by 6-inch piece of aluminum foil. Invite children to predict what drops will look like and how they might move when they are on the foil. Ask: "What shape do you think drops will make on this foil? Why do you think that?"

> **TEACHER NOTE:** This time I put a limit on the number of materials: I asked that children use just one piece of waxed paper, aluminum foil, and paper towel each. Limiting the papers seemed to help focus children on comparisons.

Again, encourage children to use movement or a whiteboard to share their predictions and ideas.

Encourage children to test out their ideas during choice time. Every few days, use morning meeting to introduce a new piece of material for children to use as they explore drops. Ask children to share their ideas about how drops might move on the new material, and then invite them to compare the new paper to ones they've been using. In addition to aluminum foil, we recommend waxed paper, paper towels, and plastic wrap. Drops created on these materials will differ in their shape and movement.

EXPLORE

Support the ongoing exploration and comparison of drops on different surfaces, until all interested children have participated.

Observe children's exploration of drops on surfaces.

Use observation record forms, sketches, and, if possible, a camera to record what children are noticing about the shape and behavior of drops on different surfaces. Observe and record the following:

- What do they notice about the shape and movement of drops on different surfaces?

- Are they noticing whether drops combine differently on different surfaces?

- What do they do to make drops of different sizes on different surfaces?

- Do they notice that water doesn't make drops on some surfaces?

- Do they explore how drops move on different surfaces by tipping the materials the drops are on?

Focus and extend children's work as they explore at the water center.

As you visit the water center, describe what you would like children to notice. For example, you might say the following:

- *Look at how fast that drop is moving over the waxed paper!*

- *After you dragged your eyedropper through the drop, it wasn't round anymore. I wonder why?*

- *What is different about the shape of drops on the aluminum foil?*

If children seem stuck on one or two ways of exploring drops on new surfaces, quietly join them and model one or two new ideas. Children ready for a new way to explore may imitate you. Try not to introduce more than one or two new ways to explore drops on surfaces at one sitting. You might try the following:

- Making very small drops

- Making drops that are close together but don't touch

TEACHER NOTE: I watched Zack make drops on waxed paper. When he made a statement about what he was noticing, I responded to see if I could find out more about what he was thinking.

> **Zack:** *They don't leave a picture after.*
>
> **Teacher:** *Why do you think that is?*
>
> **Zack:** *They slip.*
>
> **Teacher:** *So, when drops slip they don't leave tracks?*
>
> **Zack:** *Nope.*
>
> **Teacher:** *Show me drops that do make tracks.*

Zack took a piece of paper towel and dropped water in three places.

> **Zack:** *See?*
>
> **Teacher:** *Why do you think that is?*
>
> **Zack:** *This (paper towel) sucks it up.*
>
> **Teacher:** *And the waxed paper?*
>
> **Zack:** *It doesn't.*

TEACHER NOTE: As my children moved drops around on different surfaces, they developed a few phrases to describe the different ways the drops were moving. The drops that moved "like glue" were slow. The ones that moved "like JELL-O" were wiggly. The ones that were absorbed "disappeared" or "were sucked up."

- Holding your eyedropper up high above the paper and seeing what happens when you make drops
- Tipping your paper and making drops go from one side of the paper to the other without falling off

Some children will welcome or even initiate conversations about their explorations. Use these opportunities to help them notice and compare the shapes and movements their drops make on various surfaces by making comments and asking questions such as the following:

- *Which drops look the roundest . . . the ones on the plate or the ones on the foil?*
- *Which drops move the fastest . . . the ones on the plate or the ones on the foil?*
- *What happens to the drops when you fold the foil in half and then open it up again?*
- *Can you make a drop on the very edge of the waxed paper? What happens when you make a drop on the very edge of the paper towel?*

Encourage children to represent their exploration of drops.

Offer children a few ways to represent their observations and experiences. Some children like to draw—provide clipboards, paper, and markers at the water center so they can draw when they're ready. Other children prefer using playdough or clay because it replicates the three-dimensional nature of drops.

As children complete their representations, engage them in conversation with questions such as the following:

- *What shape was this drop?*
- *What kind of paper was it on? How did it move?*
- *How is it different from other drops you've made? What do you think makes it different?*

Create a documentation panel.

Using your sketches, photographs, children's representations, and excerpts from their conversations, create a documentation panel that shows children noticing the shapes drops make on different surfaces and the different ways they move on those surfaces. Cover it with plastic and hang it near the water table so children can refer to it as they play.

You will also use the panel during upcoming science talks and to share with families and colleagues.

EXTEND

Observe drops on different surfaces on rainy days.

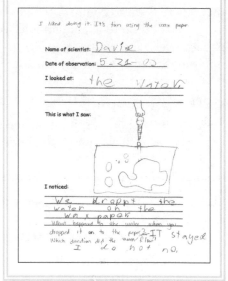

TEACHER NOTE: Some of my children love to draw and write. We've begun writing back and forth to one another about what they notice drops doing.

Take children outdoors on a rainy day.

Rainy days provide children with opportunities to observe water drops on many different surfaces. Before taking them outside, ask children to predict what raindrops will look like on objects they will see, such as a slide, the sidewalk, or the grass. Once the children have put on their raincoats, invite them to predict what the rain will look like and what it will do when it lands on their coats. Tell children you will be taking them outside to find out what raindrops really look like on their coats and on things outside. If possible, take a camera to photograph drops on the objects and children's coats.

Back inside, perhaps over lunch, talk with children about how drops looked and moved on various objects and their coats. Ask questions such as the following:

- *What happened to the rain that landed on your jacket?*
- *Of all the drops you've been making and looking at, which ones moved like the ones on your raincoat?*

Print or develop any photographs you took. Show them to children during morning meeting or as part of a science talk and discuss the differences and similarities between drops on different surfaces.

REFLECT

In small groups, reflect at the water center near the end of choice time. Meet with the whole group to reflect during a science talk.

Conduct small group discussions during choice time.

During choice time, spend a few minutes at the water center with a group of explorers and help them summarize their findings. Bring a clipboard, paper, and pencil, or a whiteboard or chart paper and record in pictures and words children's responses to questions such as the following:

- *Which materials are best for making really round drops?*
- *Which materials are not good for making drops? What happens when you drop water on them?*
- *Which materials are best for moving drops around? How are they alike?*
- *Which material do you think would make the best raincoats? How are they alike? Why do you think that?*

Conduct weekly science talks with the whole group.

Invite children to share what they have been noticing about the ways drops move and look on different papers and what they think causes the differences. Refer the group to a representational drawing, your documentation panel, one of your sketches, or a photograph from the exploration. Record children's ideas on the chart labeled "How Drops Move on Different Materials."

Use comments and questions such as the following to focus the conversation on the differences among drops: their sizes, shapes, and the way they move.

TEACHER NOTE: Today was our second science talk that focused on children's ideas about what causes drops to move differently on various materials. Nelly asked to see the box of materials and took out a piece of waxed paper and a rigid plastic plate. She held up the waxed paper and said "fastest," and then she held up the plastic plate and said "second fastest."

We put the two materials in the middle of our circle, and then I asked the group which material they thought was the third fastest. Some children thought the aluminum foil was the third fastest, and others thought it was the plastic wrap. Joe got an eyedropper and a cup of water and tested the two. By the end of our science talk, we had lined up materials in order, from fastest to slowest.

Teacher: *"What's the same about the materials that are the fastest?"*

Child: *"They're shiny. They're smooth."*

Teacher: *"What's the same about the materials that make slow-moving drops?"*

Child: *"They're bumpy."*

Teacher: *"Let's look around for other materials to test this week so we can see if all bumpy ones make slow drops and all shiny smooth ones make drops move fast."*

- *What shapes did drops make on the foil? Paper towel? Fabric? Waxed paper?*

- *Why do you think they didn't all make the same shape?*

- *How do you make a really rounded drop? A flat drop? How do you make a very tiny drop? A very big drop?*

- *How did the drops move on the foil? Paper towel? Fabric? Waxed paper?*

- *Which materials made the drops move the fastest? The slowest? Why do you think that is?*

focused exploration: sinking and floating

Certainly children have noticed that some of the objects they play with in water sink, some float, and a few stay submerged partway down. Whether an object sinks or floats has to do with the relationship between its density and the density of water. But density is too complex a concept for three-, four-, and five-year-olds to grasp. Young children can begin to notice, however, that an object's shape can affect its ability to float. For example, a hunk of steel doesn't float, but if that same hunk of steel is fashioned into a boat, it can. Of course, there are some materials that float no matter their shape—such as Styrofoam and balsa wood. Then there are objects that begin as floaters, such as pieces of cloth and plastic cups with holes, that eventually sink because they absorb water or take on water through their holes. The following focus on sinking and floating is important because it gives children a variety of experiences that, when combined with reflection, help children begin to form ideas about this phenomenon.

Step 1: Test Objects to See if They Sink or Float

Objects don't always behave the way we think they will when we put them in water. After all, grapes sink and grapefruits don't! By exploring and reflecting, children can begin to develop their own ideas about why some objects float in water and others do not. Isolating this property of water from other aspects of water play helps children focus on the relationship between the shape of an object or the material it is made of, and whether it floats or not.

CORE EXPERIENCES

☐ Talk about their experiences with sinking and floating.

☐ Participate in a demonstration of sink and float.

☐ Test objects to see if they sink or float.

☐ Begin to develop theories about why some objects sink and why other objects float.

PREPARATION

☐ Display books about sinking and floating around the classroom.

☐ Plan to keep the water table open for children's continued exploration of flow or streams.

SCHEDULE

☐ 10–15 minutes for a demonstration with the whole group

☐ 45–60 minutes for choice time, four or five times during the week

☐ 10–15 minutes for a discussion with the whole group

MATERIALS

Chart: "Our Ideas about Sinking and Floating"

At the Water Center

☐ Clear tubs of water

☐ Clipboards, paper, and markers

☐ Chart paper or whiteboard to record results

☐ A selection of eight or more objects for children to test (Be sure to include objects that might surprise children. For example, a pumpkin floats and a grape sinks; a metal cake pan floats and a penny sinks.)

FAMILY CONNECTION

Send a note home to families telling them about the sink and float tests their children are doing in class. Explain the way children are predicting, testing, and recording their results. Suggest families conduct some tests of their own at home, record their results, and send their data into class so their children can share their experiences with their peers.

TEACHING PLAN

ENGAGE

Lead a discussion and demonstration with the whole group lasting ten to fifteen minutes to introduce the focus on sinking and floating.

> Many children jump to the conclusion that heavy objects sink and light objects float. While it can be tempting to point out that heavy ocean liners float, and paper clips sink, it's best to help children challenge and refine their theories by providing a variety of heavy and light objects for them to put in water, as well as allowing them the time they need to collect and analyze their data.

Discuss children's previous experiences.

Gather the whole group together in a circle and ask the following questions:

- *What do we mean when we say "float"? Can you give me an example?*

- *What about the word "sink"? What does that mean?*

Continue the conversation with questions such as the following to find out more about children's experiences observing or playing with objects that sink or float.

- *What can you think of that goes to the bottom, or sinks, in the bathtub or a sink full of water?*

- *What can you think of that stays at the top of, or floats, in water?*

- *What things have you seen that sink very quickly? Slowly?*

- *What things have you seen that float for awhile and then start to sink? Why do you think they do that?*

Make predictions and test them.

- Put the clear container of water on a small table or in front of you so all children can easily see it.

- Show children an object (such as a metal spoon) and invite them to tell what they think will happen to it when you put it in the water and why they think so.

Record results.

- Use a whiteboard or chart paper to sketch and label the object (with a spoon, for example, write "Sinkers" as a heading).

- As you test one or two other objects, record your results in this manner.

Review procedures for doing sink and float tests during choice time.

Tell the children that during choice time they can test other objects to see if they sink or float. Show them the container of objects you collected for this purpose. Explain that the objects, the container of water, and the whiteboard or chart paper will be at the water center. Remind the children that they can record their results so the whole group will know what happened. Also mention that the water table will be open during choice time.

ISSUE: *My children say they've done this before.*

RESPONSE: Most children become reengaged once they have new objects to test. Others may want to try to get a 2-inch piece of pliable plasticine (or other oil-based clay) to float by changing its shape.

EXPLORE

Test objects at the water center.

Facilitate sink and float tests.

Help children focus on their tests with strategies such as the following:

- Show children one object at a time, ask for their prediction, and then hand them the object to test. Remind them to record their result on the whiteboard or chart paper.

- Have children at the water center take turns testing objects so they can notice what their friends are finding out.

- As children test objects, suggest a way they can record their results. Provide a whiteboard, some chart paper, or two trays marked "sinkers" and "floaters," and have children place objects they've tested on the appropriate one.

Acknowledge children's work with comments such as the following:

- *You are watching the crayon so carefully!*

- *Find an object that you think will float. Why do you think it will float? Find one you think will sink.*

Some children will want to talk about the results of their tests. Help them articulate theories about what makes some objects sink and others float by asking questions such as the following:

- *What do you think made it float? Sink?*

- *You said you thought it would float because it's round. Do you think all round things float? How can you find out?*

- *What is it made out of? Do you think all things made out of the same material float? How can you find out?*

Record children's responses so you can refer to them during science talks.

Suggest children make one of their "sinkers" into a "floater," or they might want to try the opposite—make a "floater" into a "sinker."

Observe and document children's exploration.

Observe children as they test objects, and note behaviors or conversations that provide some evidence of their developing understanding of sinking and floating. Observe and document the following:

- Are children surprised by what an object does when it is placed in water? Do they expect the same object to respond the same way each time it's put in water?

- What kinds of reasons are they giving for why some objects sink and others float?

Sketch or photograph some objects as they sink or float. You will use these documents to facilitate science talks and to make a documentation panel.

ISSUE: *How can I spend all of this time at the water center facilitating children's sink and float experiments?*

RESPONSE: If possible, plan in advance to have your assistant and a parent volunteer focus on the other children during choice time while you work at the water center, or show an assistant or volunteer what to do.

Children typically theorize that heavy objects sink and lighter ones don't. Instead of encouraging or correcting this misconception, provide children with objects and opportunities to examine their theory further. Include heavy objects that float and light ones that sink at the water table, and as children test them, probe their thinking with a question such as the following:

- *You were saying that you thought the grapefruit would sink because it's so heavy. But it's floating! What a surprise! Why do you think that happened?*

It's important that children continue to question and test their assumptions.

This is a good time to model looking at the side of the tub of water as objects sink or float. As you sketch the results of some of the sink and float tests, draw this side view and include a line to represent the water level in each of your drawings.

Create a documentation panel.

Use your sketches or photographs, a copy of the records children have been making on a whiteboard or chart paper, and excerpts from children's conversations about their sink and float tests to create a documentation panel describing the process children are using to test objects to see if they sink or float.

Or create a panel that profiles the process of one child as she develops a theory of sinking and floating. For example, you might document a child's investigation beginning with her declaration that light things float, and continue the panel with pictures and words describing how she found out that some lightweight things sink.

EXTEND

Watch objects sink and float outdoors.

Throw leaves, sticks, and rocks into puddles or ponds.

There's something very appealing to children about throwing leaves, sticks, and stones into puddles, rivers, and ponds. You can plan an outdoor experience for children that focuses their thinking on sinking and floating while they enjoy one of their favorite activities—tossing leaves, sticks, and stones into water. Perhaps you are lucky enough to be within walking distance of a pond or river; if not, wait for a rainy day to provide your children with puddles.

Before heading outdoors, tell the children that you will be taking them to a puddle, pond, or river so they can do more sink and float tests. Ask them to tell you about any experiences they've had putting things into puddles, rivers, lakes, and so forth.

Brainstorm together some of the items they might try throwing in the puddles, pond, or river, and invite children to predict if each object will sink or float. Take a clipboard, paper, and pen to record what happens as children toss leaves, sticks, and rocks into the water.

Back indoors, over lunch or during the next day's morning meeting, discuss with children the results of their outdoor sink and float tests. Ask questions such as the following:

- *What happened when you put a leaf in the pond? Did anyone have something different happen when they put a leaf in the pond? Why do you think that is?*

- *What do you think makes some sticks float and other sticks sink?*

- *Do you think there are rocks that float? What makes you say that?*

> **TEACHER NOTE:** After our walk to the pond, we ate lunch and talked about the different things children threw into the water. Doris declared that all rocks sink. When we asked her why she was so convinced that all rocks sink, she said, "Because they're heavy." Then Alex reminded her that our pumpkin floats. I'm going to ask the other teachers to see if anyone has some floating volcanic rock (such as pumice) I can borrow for Doris to explore.

REFLECT

Share experiences and discuss theories about sinking and floating.

Conduct a science talk with the whole group.

Begin the science talk by showing children a pile of objects they've been testing at the water center. Pick up one of the objects and say: "Here's a tennis ball. It floated when you put it in the tub of water. Why do you think it floats?"

Accept any answers children give. Also, focus their thinking on the shape and material of the objects with questions such as the following:

- *What do you think is important about that shape that helps it float?*

- *How do you think the metal (or wood, plastic, and so on) it's made of helps it float? Sink?*

- *How do you think the way you put it in the tub of water helped it float? Sink?*

Use sketches and words to record children's ideas on a chart labeled: "Our Ideas about Sinking and Floating."

Step 2: Rigid Tubes

When children place an object in a tub of water, it sinks, floats, or stays suspended. Children can observe the ways objects sink and float in a more dramatic way when rigid tubes are filled with water and small objects, then capped and turned upside down—some objects fall to the bottom, others float down, and some move up! Air bubbles also rise to the surface, which can affect how certain materials move through the tube. With the help of these materials, children focus their observations and thinking even further on what makes some objects sink and others float.

CORE EXPERIENCES

☐ Observe how objects and air move through water-filled rigid tubes.

☐ Represent observations.

☐ Continue to develop ideas related to sinking and floating.

PREPARATION

Plan to keep the water table open so children can continue their focus on flow or streams.

SCHEDULE

☐ 5–10 minutes for a demonstration during a whole group meeting

☐ 45–60 minutes for choice time, four or five times during the week

☐ 10–15 minutes for a discussion with the whole group

EXAMPLE:

OUR IDEAS ABOUT WHY THE PUMPKIN FLOATS AND THE PAPER CLIP SINKS

KYLE: The pumpkin is round and can bounce around in the water.

KASSANDRA: The paper clip has places the water goes through; not the pumpkin.

OREOLUWA: The paper clip is made of metal and the pumpkin isn't.

OREOLUWA: Like Kassandra said, the paper clip has holes in it.

MATERIALS

While children observe objects in rigid tubes at the water center, they continue a focus on flow or streams at the water table.

At the Water Center

☐ Tubs of water

☐ Funnels

☐ Cups without holes

☐ Four or more rigid tubes with end caps

☐ Eight or more of the following:

- Objects that fit into the rigid tubes and float in water (Examples include pieces of Styrofoam, pieces of sticks, most sequins, most rubber bands, and pieces of plastic straws.)

- Objects that fit into the rigid tubes and sink slowly in water (Examples include most buttons, tiddlywinks, and glitter.)

- Objects that fit into the rigid tubes and sink quickly in water (Examples include marbles, pennies, pebbles, nails, and metal paper clips.)

FAMILY CONNECTION

Send a note home to families suggesting they work with their children on the following activity. Make an object that usually floats into one that sinks; then, make an object that usually sinks into one that will float. Suggest children bring these items to class to share with their friends.

TEACHING PLAN

ENGAGE

Introduce rigid tubes in a meeting with the whole group.

Rigid tube demonstration.

Show the children an empty rigid tube with one end capped. Demonstrate how you want children to put together and use the tubes.

- Put two to five small objects in a tube.

- Hold the tube over a tub of water and fill it to 2 inches from the top using a funnel and a cup.

- Cap the top with a second end cap.

- Describe what you see happening as a way of modeling descriptive language. For example, you might say the following:
  - *The rubber band is moving back and forth from one side of the tube to the other as it slowly sinks down.*
  - *The yellow wooden bead popped right up to the top!*
  - *Look what happens when the bubble bangs into the paper clip!*

Turn the tube upside down again and encourage children to talk about what they see happening. Help them notice that some objects go to the top of the tube and others go to the bottom. Encourage children to describe their observations with questions such as the following:

- *Which things are going up? Which ones are going down?*

- *How is the penny moving?*

Help children notice the different speeds and paths objects take as they move up and down by asking questions such as the following:

- *Are the paper clip and the sequin moving the same way? How are they moving differently?*

- *Why do you think the sequin doesn't go straight down?*

- *Which of these other objects might float back and forth like the tiddly-winks? Why do you say that?*

Introduce routines for exploring sinking and floating with rigid tubes at the water center.

Invite two children to demonstrate a way they can help each other fill a tube. Suggest one child hold a tube while the other uses a funnel and a cup to fill it with water. Provide a tray to catch spills.

Ask children to choose some objects to put into the tube, and then cap the tube. Show children how to hold the tube by putting their hands over the end caps and pressing in a bit, to keep the caps from popping off.

EXPLORE

Support children's exploration during choice times, until all children have participated.

Observe and document children's exploration.

An important aspect to look for is children's ideas about what makes some objects sink and others float. Use an observation form to record what you see children do or what you hear them say about what makes objects sink or float. Record and observe the following:

- Do they focus on the size, shape, or material of the object when they try to explain why it sinks or why it floats?

- Are they refining their theories by testing additional objects?

If possible, audiotape or videotape children's exploration. Review the tapes and add notes to your observation form. Video clips of children turning tubes over and reacting to their observations can also provide stimuli for science talks.

Talk with children about their explorations.

As children observe objects in the rigid tubes, ask them what they are noticing. If they are eager to respond, continue to engage them in

> **TEACHER NOTE:** At first I asked children to show with their hands how certain objects moved down through the tubes. But then Clarissa picked up a rubber band and held it as she moved it slowly—zigzagging down through the air as if it were in a tube of water. From then on, most children chose to actually hold the object they wanted to represent as it moved through water.

> **TEACHER NOTE:** Most children need adult help to put the cap on the end of a water-filled tube.

conversation with questions such as the following:

- *Henry, what seems to move the slowest in your tube?*
- *Does it move more slowly than the glitter in Skyler's tube?*
- *What do you think is going to happen to the shell when you turn the tube upside down? What makes you say that?*
- *What's happening to the button? Why do you think it isn't going straight down?*
- *The acorn is racing with the paper clip! Which one do you think will win? Why do you say that?*

Provide additional activities that challenge children in their exploration of water. Some ideas include the following:

- Find an object children think will sink; find one they think will float.
- Create a tube of objects that all move up, or one in which they all move down.
- Create a tube of objects that move slowly (or quickly).

Children typically notice bubbles in rigid tubes. Help them notice how these bubbles behave by asking questions such as the following:

- *What is the bubble doing?*
- *Does it always do that?*
- *Can you make it move slower? Faster?*
- *Can you make more bubbles? Bigger ones? Smaller ones?*
- *Where do you think the bubble came from? What makes you say that?*

Encourage representation.

Suggest children show with their fingers or hands how an object or a bubble moves through water in their tube.

Invite children to draw what's happening inside their tubes. Suggest they begin by representing just one or two objects. You might provide children with predrawn outlines of rigid tubes to facilitate the representation of the objects.

Encourage children to use objects like those in their tubes to demonstrate how they move in water. Hand one object to a child and ask him to move it in the air the way it moves in his tube.

Create a documentation panel.

Use your sketches or photographs, children's drawings, and excerpts from transcripts to create a documentation panel showing how chil-

---

TEACHER NOTE: Carmen was more interested in which objects floated up than in which ones sunk to the bottom. I took this picture and shared it with her the next day. That's when I asked: Why do you think this bead didn't sink?

TEACHER NOTE: John and Dayvian both chose to put rubber bands in their rigid tubes. John's stuck to the side of his tube, and Dayvian's stayed in a circle shape and floated up. As we were comparing the two, Dayvian noticed a bubble in his tube. He moved his "wand" slowly, keeping his eye on the bubble. Then John noticed a bubble in his tube. The bubble was stuck to the bottom of his rubber band, moving it up!

John: *The rubber band goes up and the bubble catches it inside—then the bubble pops and the elastics get away.*

John turned his tube over and created more bubbles. He spent about five minutes doing this, watching the bubbles float up.

John: *They're trying to swim back up.*

dren are developing theories about what makes some objects sink and others float.

If possible, include their theories related to how an object's shape and the material it's made from affect its buoyancy. You will use the panel during the upcoming science talk.

REFLECT

During choice time and science talks, encourage children to share what they notice about objects moving up and down in rigid tubes of water.

Conduct discussions with small groups during choice time.

A few minutes before choice time is over, sit with children at the water center and help them summarize some of their findings. Use a clipboard or chart paper to record their ideas and responses to questions such as the following:

- *Which objects always float up?*
- *Which objects always sink down?*
- *How can you tell if an object is going to go up or if it's going to go down?*
- *Are there objects that sometimes float up and other times sink down? Why do you think that is?*

Conduct weekly science talks with the whole group.

Bring a documentation panel, children's representations, your photographs, or filled rigid tubes to a science talk with the whole group. Ask children what they now believe makes objects float.

Record children's ideas in pictures and words on a chart labeled "Our Ideas about Sinking and Floating." Use questions such as the following to probe children's thinking:

- *What about the object's shape? Does that make a difference? Why do you say that?*
- *What about the materials the object is made with? Does that make a difference? Why do you say that?*

Some children might want to add additional ideas to the chart. Create subheads such as "Why Some Things Float Up Faster than Others" or "Why Some Things Sink Faster than Others."

TEACHER NOTE: I had a four-year-old and a five-year-old show interest in drawing what happened in their rigid tubes. Both represented something they noticed about the bubbles they saw floating up.

Step 3: Boats

Boats are supposed to float, but they don't always stay above water. By incorporating boat building and sailing into a focus on sinking and floating, you provide children with a dramatic context for their exploration, and a chance to actually make something float rather than find something that floats. As you focus children on the shapes and materials that make "good" boats and introduce them to real boats in books, on the Web, or in your neighborhood, you will be helping them develop their ideas about floating and sinking even further.

CORE EXPERIENCES

☐ Share experiences making, seeing, and riding in boats.

☐ Hear about materials for building boats at the water center.

☐ Build and sail boats.

☐ Formulate ideas about how shapes and materials affect a boat's ability to float.

PREPARATION

☐ Create an area for making boats near the water table.

☐ Take other materials out of the water table so it has room to float boats.

☐ Create a classroom display of image books and other books about boats.

☐ Choose a storybook that features a boat carrying people, animals, or other cargo to read to the group as an introduction to the focus on boats. (See suggestions below.)

SCHEDULE

☐ 10–15 minutes for a "read aloud" with the whole group

☐ 45–60 minutes for choice time, four or five times a week

☐ 10–15 minutes for a discussion with the whole group, once a week

MATERIALS

☐ Copies of the observation record form (p. 116)

☐ Charts: "Important Ideas for Making Good Boats," "Good Shapes for Boats," "Good Materials for Boats," "How the Boat(s) We Saw Keep from Sinking"

At the Water Table

☐ Clean, empty yogurt containers

☐ Styrofoam meat trays that have been washed with very hot, soapy water

☐ Pieces of corrugated and shirt-weight cardboard

☐ Cardboard rolls from paper towels

☐ Plasticine

☐ Aluminum foil

☐ Straws

☐ Different kinds of paper

☐ Items children can use as cargo (examples include toy cars and people, stuffed animals, or math manipulatives)

At the Water Center

Children continue their focus on sinking and floating by using rigid tubes to explore objects in water and by testing objects in tubs of water.

Family Connection

Send a note home telling families about the focus on boat-building materials and designs. Suggest they offer their children a few recycled materials so they can build and sail a boat at home. Also, invite the children to bring their boats to class to share with their friends.

Teaching Plan

Engage

Introduce the focus on boats.

Discuss children's previous experiences.

Gather the whole group together and invite them to share their personal experiences with boats—making them, riding in them, and seeing them. Focus the group on the fact that boats are made to float by asking a question such as: "Why do you think boats don't sink?"

Read a story that features a boat.

Read a storybook about a boat carrying people, animals, or other cargo to the whole group: for example, John Burningham's *Mr. Gumpy's Outing* or Pamela Allen's *Who Sank the Boat?*

As you discuss the book, help children think about sinking and floating with questions such as the following:

- *Why do you think the boat floated?*

- *What made it (or might make it) sink?*

- *What do you think helps it float, even with so many animals?*

Introduce supplies and procedures for making boats.

Tell children that they will have opportunities to make boats and float them in the water table. Show them some of the materials for making boats you've collected, and introduce the idea of cargo by referring to the book you read and showing children the toy animals or math manipulatives you've collected for that purpose. Help children think about building boats that are "sea-worthy" by asking questions such as the following:

- *What kinds of boats do you think you will make?*
- *How will you keep your boats from sinking?*

EXPLORE

Make and test boats for as long as children are interested.

Observe and document the decisions children make as they choose materials and designs to make boats that float and carry cargo.

Listen for ideas children have about what makes a "good" boat and record them on an observation form. Observe and record the following:

- Sketch or photograph the kinds of boats children construct.
- Jot down the ways children alter the shape of their boats.
- Make note of the materials they choose to use for building their boats and any comments they might make about why they make their choices.

Use your notes to help facilitate upcoming science talks.

Encourage children to talk about their ideas for boat building.

As you visit the water table, ask children to tell you about their boats. With children who are interested in continuing a conversation, ask questions that help them examine their ideas about what makes a good boat. For example, you might ask the following:

- *What are you doing to make sure it won't sink?*
- *What will your boat be able to carry?*
- *What did you use to make your boat? Why did you choose that material?*
- *What do you think will happen to your boat when you put it in the water?*
- *What shape is your boat? Why did you choose to make it that shape?*
- *What do you think will happen to your boat when you put people or animals in it? Can you make a boat that holds even more animals?*

Record children's ideas in pictures and words on charts or on an observation form.

TEACHER NOTE: Katherine predicted that her boat would float fine—she'd made it out of two boxes, a smaller one on top of a larger one, and it floated nicely. Samuel's boat took on water right away. His boat's hull was made from molded composite cardboard; water found its way into the molded nooks and crannies. He observed carefully as water seeped in and sunk his boat. Alessandro's boat was also made with molded composite cardboard. It carried pennies. At first his boat hovered just below the surface.

Alessandro: *It's not floating, but it's not sinking either.*

After a minute, his boat did sink.

ISSUE: *A few of my children are getting frustrated because their boats never float.*

RESPONSE: Help these children figure out why their boats sink—perhaps they're using materials that are too absorbent? Designs that are top heavy? Hulls that are too flat? After you've diagnosed the problem, help children make changes by either offering new materials that aren't as absorbent, or helping them design boats that have sides and aren't too tall.

Support children as they record the amount of cargo their boats carry.

Help children keep track of the number of animals, people, or whatever cargo that their boats can carry without sinking. You might try the following:

- Count aloud with children who need support.
- Use tally marks on a piece of paper to record amounts, or teach children to record with tally marks for their friends.

Encourage representation.

Suggest children draw or paint representations of their boats as the boats sit in the water. Pull a chair or two up to the water table and offer children clipboards, paper and markers, or an easel and paints to use to draw their boat floating in water. Encourage children to add marks that represent their cargo, and a line that represents the water level on the boats' hulls.

EXTEND

Help children make connections to real boats.

Visit a harbor or dock.

Before the trip, engage children in a discussion about boats by asking questions such as the following:

- *What is special or unique about boats?*
- *What are they used for? How do they keep from sinking?*

When you are at the harbor or dock, record children's answers to the following questions:

- *How do these boats keep from sinking?*
- *What are they made of?*
- *What shapes are they?*
- *What are the boats carrying? How does the boat carry these heavy things?*

Suggest children sit and use clipboards, paper, and markers to draw a boat as it sits in the water.

After the visit, perhaps over lunch, review the children's predictions by referring to your charts, and create a new chart labeled: "How the Boat(s) We Saw Keep from Sinking."

Invite a sailor into the classroom.

Talk with the guest sailor ahead of time and tell her a bit about the children's exploration of sink and float. Brainstorm items she might be able to bring into the classroom that are designed to float and to be used by sailors, such as life jackets, buoys, and so forth.

After the visit, perhaps over lunch, ask the children to think about how life jackets and buoys float.

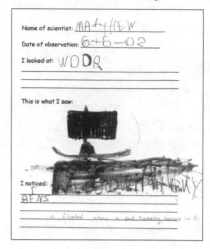

EXAMPLE: This is an example of one child's representation of his boat and the beans he put in it as "cargo."

ISSUE: *I'm afraid my children will begin competing about whose boat holds the most cargo, and I don't like to encourage competition.*

RESPONSE: Try to keep the emphasis on the boat and its capacity for holding cargo. For example, you might say, "Which boat holds the most cargo?" instead of "Whose boat holds the most cargo?"

REFLECT

Use whole group and small group science talks as a way for children to reflect on their exploration of sink and float.

Conduct weekly science talks with the whole group.

Invite children to bring their boats to a science talk. Put the boats in the middle of the rug or on a table so everyone can see.

Use the boats, a documentation panel, photographs, or children's representational drawings to facilitate a conversation about what designs and materials help make boats float and carry things. Ask questions such as the following:

- *Tell us about one of your good boats.*
- *How much cargo can or did it hold?*
- *What shapes are these "good" boats?*
- *What did you use to make these "good" boats?*
- *What about your boats that didn't float? What do you think you learned from them? How might you change them so they could float?*

As they share their ideas, extend children's thinking by encouraging them to provide evidence based on their own observations and experiences. For example, you might say the following:

- *What makes you say that a flat-bottomed boat is good for holding cargo? Can you tell us what happened when you put cargo in a flat-bottomed boat?*
- *Why do you say that Styrofoam makes good boats? Tell us what happened when you built a boat from Styrofoam. What materials did you try using that didn't work?*

Record children's theories.

Begin the discussion with a question: "What is important to remember if you want to make a good boat?" Follow up with questions such as the following:

- *What materials would you choose to make a good boat?*
- *What shapes make good boats for holding a lot of cargo?*

Use the charts labeled "Good Shapes for Boats" and "Good Materials for Boats" to record children's ideas in pictures and words.

> The relationship between a boat's shape, the material it's made from, the kind and amount of cargo it's carrying, and where that cargo is placed, affects whether or not a boat floats. This relationship is too complex for young children to understand fully, but they should be encouraged to develop theories about what makes a good boat. They should also be encouraged to explain their theories and support them with evidence.

Wrapping Up

Children have had many experiences exploring water with different materials, focusing on its various properties. They have observed, predicted, tested, recorded, and discussed the ways water behaves. There are many ways you can help children reflect upon and celebrate their explorations. As children share their experiences with each other and with their families, they will gain a deeper understanding of the concepts and inquiry skills that have been central to their exploration.

CORE EXPERIENCES

☐ Plan ways to share the water exploration with family and friends.

☐ Make a class book about an aspect of the exploration.

☐ Host an open house.

PREPARATION

☐ Check with your staff and administration, and identify a date for hosting an hour-long open house to share children's experiences.

☐ Ask children to decorate invitations for families and friends.

☐ Collect the charts, documentation panels, class books, drawings and collages, and other documents the class created during "Exploring Water." Display them, along with children's favorite books about boats, rivers, and water, around the classroom.

SCHEDULE

☐ 5–10 minutes for a planning meeting a few days before the open house, and again for about an hour before the open house.

MATERIALS

☐ Oak tag (enough for each child to make a page for a class book)

☐ A guest book for family and friends to write their comments at the open house

TEACHING PLAN

ENGAGE

Introduce the open house in a meeting with the whole group for five to ten minutes.

Create a class book.

During a meeting with the whole group, tell the children that they will be working together to make a book about their water exploration. Help them choose one or more foci for the book, or choose one you think they are most interested in. Some suggestions include the following:

- Ways We Moved Water from One Tub to Another
- What Happens to Drops on Different Surfaces
- Rainy-Day Walks and What We Noticed
- Our Sink and Float Tests
- Boats that Float

Explain that the writing area will be open for the next few days for children to make pages for the book.

Help children plan for the open house.

Gather your group together. Explain that you would like to plan an open house so they can share with their families and friends some of the things they've done and learned while exploring water. Ask the children what experiences they would like to share with their guests. Record their ideas, using words and pictures, on a chart.

Discuss the role of "host."

Help children anticipate what the open house will be like and how they can act as hosts. Together, list the many things children can do with their guests:

- Use rigid tubes
- Make drops
- Make boats
- Use the Velcro pegboard
- Use tubing and the wire water wall
- Look at documentation panels
- Read class books

Involve children in helping you set up the classroom for the open house.

CONDUCT THE WATER EXPLORATION OPEN HOUSE

As you welcome your guests, point out the guest book. Ask them to write a comment about what they do and what they see during the open house.

extension activities

The focus of *Exploring Water with Young Children* is on children's first-hand experiences with water in and around the classroom. However, this kind of exploration is not the only way children can learn about the physical properties of water. As children explore, you can enrich and broaden their experiences and learning by taking them outdoors to observe water on a rainy day, in a fountain, or in a stream. You can introduce them to people who work with water, and share relevant books and photographs.

We suggest that you do an extension activity about once a week during focused exploration.

Take a Field Trip

Observing water in a variety of settings can add to children's developing ideas about the properties of water. Field trips provide opportunities to compare how water behaves in the water table with how it behaves in a stream or fountain. Field trip destinations for exploring water do not have to be exotic, as water's properties can be observed in many places.

SUGGESTED DESTINATIONS

- Outside the classroom during or immediately following a rain shower

- Streams, rivers, or ponds

- Fountains

- Bottling companies (for example, soft drinks)

PREPARATION

- As with any field trip, it is a good idea to visit the site ahead of time. Make sure it will be a safe location for children.

- If you plan to take children outside during or after it rains, you might go on a walk during or after a rain shower first yourself. Look for streams of water, and make note of things such as where those streams are fast and where they are slow.

- If you plan to take children outside while it's raining, be sure you will have enough raincoats or umbrellas on hand to keep children as dry as possible.

BEFORE THE TRIP

- Arrange for adult volunteers to join you on the trip. Plan a time to talk with them about what will happen on the trip, your expectations for what children might engage with, and the way they can support children at the site. (For example: share what the children have been doing and talking about so they have an idea of some of the properties of water that might be observed, and give them a list of questions they can ask to focus children's observations.)

- Consider alerting children to one part of the trip, such as water running through gutters and downspouts, or what happens to drops of rain on different surfaces. Suggest particulars they can look for (such as, "I wonder where the water goes off of the roof" or "I wonder if the water will come out of the fountain in drops or streams").

- While children will notice lots of things at the site you choose to visit, you may want to provide a focus. You might ask the children a question or two and draw out their predictions, recording them in words and pictures. Possible questions include the following:
  - *Where do you think we'll see moving water? What do you think will be making it move?*
  - *What kinds of things do you think we might see floating in puddles? Sinking in puddles?*
  - *How do you think the water will look at the fountain?*
  - *How do you think the fountain will sound?*

DURING THE TRIP

Assign small groups of children to each teacher and adult volunteer. Encourage children to do the following:

- Observe closely.

- Describe what they notice about water.

- Record some observations by making drawings.

Connect the experience to children's classroom explorations. Ask follow-up questions to probe their thinking. For example:

- *How are the gutters different from our wire water wall?*
- *Where does the water go?*
- *Do you see drops of water anywhere?*
- *How does the water sound?*

Document what children do, say, and see so you can help them discuss and reflect on the visit later in the classroom. If you have a camera, take pictures of the children making their observations.

AFTER THE TRIP

Have a brief conversation about what you saw. Ask questions such as the following:

- *What did you like about the walk in the rain?*
- *What did you see? Hear? Smell?*

Put out drawing and art materials. Encourage children to represent the trip. Write down excerpts from their conversations.

The next day, or when your photos have been developed, use children's observational drawings, videotapes, audiotapes, and/or photos and documentation panels as reflection tools to discuss the questions you focused on during the visit. Probe children's reflective thinking with questions such as the following:

- *What did you notice about the rain?*
- *Where did the water go?*
- *How did the drops look?*
- *Where did you see bubbles? What did you notice about them?*

Record children's ideas, in drawings and words, on a chart.

Invite Guests into the Classroom

Children's interest is piqued by visitors. When you introduce children to an adult who uses materials similar to the ones they have been using, such as a plumber, you are likely to stimulate new ideas in children's water play.

PREPARATION

- Send home a letter asking family members if they, or anyone they know, would be available to share an expertise, hobby, or interest related to water exploration.

- Talk with the visitor ahead of time and describe the kinds of explorations your children have been engaged in, their interests, and their questions. Suggest the visitor bring any tools she uses to show the children. Ask if she minds being photographed or videotaped.

Suggested Guests

- A plumber
- An engineer
- People who work with local water-supply offices
- People who design irrigation systems for farms or sprinkler systems for lawns

Before the Visit

Have a brief conversation with your class about what your visitor does, and ask children what they might want to learn from their guest. Write down children's questions to share with the visitor. The children may want to know more personal things such as where they live or if they have children. These questions are also important to children because they help them see the visitors as real people who use science inquiry in their daily lives.

During the Visit

Ask the visitors to talk about what they do, and invite them to share journals, tools, books, and stories related to their work. Give children a chance to ask additional questions. Share some of what children have been doing with water systems, such as the wire water wall, and photos, observational drawings, and class books of the children's experiences. If possible, take photographs or videotape the visit.

After the Visit

Have a brief conversation with your class. Ask children what they learned from the visitor and refer to photos or the video of the classroom visit, if they were made. During choice time on the following day, invite children to join you at a small table to draw pictures about the visit for a class book. Ask children about the photos or their drawings and write their words down.

Use Books to Extend the Exploration

There are many books that deal with themes that relate to the properties of water. Some entertain, some inform, some inspire. The books that inform a child's study of water need to be scientifically accurate, engaging, and informative for young children. As children move in and out of open and focused explorations, teachers can offer resources in a variety of ways to support the inquiry.

BOOKS

- Books should be integral to children's work and play, and they need to be accessible. Stories, photos, diagrams, poems, lists, and informative text each offer something unique to the process. Make a special effort to display books that have engaging pictures related to the properties of water children have been exploring. Encourage children to visit the book corner to look through these books, and encourage other adults to read to small groups or individual children.

- Recommended books to use with extension activities appear in the resources section (p. 105). Use the guidelines presented below and in the resources section to help you choose an assortment of books. In addition to having library books around the classroom, you can use different kinds of books for extension activities in different ways.

FICTION

- Fact and fantasy
- Real-life

Choose books that present or raise questions about the physical properties of water—how it flows and takes the shape of its container, that things can sink or float in it, the shapes of drops and bubbles. Then, when you read aloud each book to an individual child, a small group, or the whole group, you'll be providing a new opportunity for children to wonder about the book's setting, learn vocabulary, and focus their thinking on water concepts without disturbing the flow of the story. You might raise issues or ask questions, such as the following:

- *Why do you think the boat is lower in the water?*
- *Why do you think there's water all over the floor?*
- *Do the pictures of the drops look like the ones we've made?*

NONFICTION

- Image books—Use image books with a few children at a time, so everyone can see. Read aloud or summarize short pieces of text in response to children's interests and questions. Ask children how the images of water compare to what they've been observing:
  - *Did we find that a pin sinks or floats? The one in this picture floats.*
  - *Did we ever see water look this color? Why do you think the illustrator decided to make it look this way?*

- Information books—Use information books with small groups during choice time as you observe water. Information books will often provide accurate vocabulary and information about the properties of water.

Preview a variety of these kinds of books (see "Books and Web Sites," p. 105, for more information) and choose those that have clear images of the kinds of water phenomena children have actually been observing, as well as others they can use to compare to what they've been seeing.

BIOGRAPHY

As you read biographies aloud, look for opportunities to discuss the characters' curiosity about water, and their perseverance to continue to find out as much as possible. You may ask questions such as the following:

- *What do you think she was interested in?*
- *What questions did she ask?*
- *What did she do to try to answer the questions?*

POETRY

Poets share their feelings about nature, images, and sounds. Use poets' words to help children experience the feelings and see the images they paint with words. Read aloud a variety of poems and ask questions that help children connect their experiences to those expressed in the poetry, such as the following:

- *That poem was about a stream like the one we visited. What words did the poet use that reminded you of the stream?*
- *What words would you add?*

resources

Science Teaching

YOUNG CHILDREN'S INQUIRY

"Young Children's Inquiry" is a framework to help you think about how new knowledge is created in science. (See the chart on the following page.) It is useful whether you think about the inquiry of a scientist, your own inquiry, or the inquiry of a child. The framework suggests that the stages follow one another. To some extent they do, but the many arrows suggest that the process of inquiry is not linear, and children will move back and forth and around as they explore the world around them.

Inquiry is about questions, but it's hard for children to ask questions about something if they haven't had a chance to get to know the thing or the materials or the event, whether it is balls rolling, snails, or water flow. So the first stage in the framework is to *engage, notice, wonder and question*—it is a time for children to play, to see what they already know, to mess about in a rich environment with little direct guidance or structure. As children explore, they ask questions through words or actions. As they continue, they may be struck by a particular idea or question such as "I won-

der what would happen if I put this block here?" or "Why is the snail on the wall?"

Many of the questions children raise may not be ones that are possible or interesting to investigate. "Why is the sky blue?" cannot be explored directly. "What is the name of this plant?" will not go far. But "What are ways I can get the water to move?" is the start of a rich investigation. At this stage, children often need adult guidance to begin to *focus observations and clarify questions*. They need to be encouraged to make some predictions and guesses about what might happen.

When children engage in more focused explorations, they are entering the experimental phase of inquiry. Even very young children, given the right materials and teacher support and guidance, can *plan, predict, and take action; observe closely; collect, record, and represent experiences and data; reflect on experience; explore patterns and relationships; and construct reasonable explanations and ask new questions*. Notice that on the framework, this process goes around and around. Children may explore a question for a long time. Their explorations may lead to new questions and new investigations.

When children have a good deal of experience and begin to form some ideas, they need to be encouraged to step back from their investigative work, review and reflect on what they have done, and *share, discuss, and reflect with the group*, as well as *formulate ideas and theories*. By sharing, children have opportunities to reflect and relate their ideas and experiences to what others have done. Differences in experience may demand a return to the exploration. New questions may come up leading to new explorations.

Inquiry

Engage, notice, wonder, question

Focus observations, clarify questions

Plan, predict,
take action

Ask new
questions

Explore, investigate

Observe
closely

Reflect on experience,
explore patterns and
relationships, construct
reasonable explanations

Collect, record, represent
experiences and data

**Share, discuss, and reflect with group;
draw conclusions; formulate ideas
and theories**

THE TEACHER'S ROLE

Teachers play a number of major roles when exploring science with children. This section includes such responsibilities as the following:

- Create a science-rich environment
- Engage children in science explorations
- Focus and deepen children's experiences and thinking

Observing and assessing, which is also important, will be described in the next section.

CREATE A SCIENCE-RICH ENVIRONMENT

One of the most important roles you play in this exploration is creating an environment and culture that supports and encourages children as water explorers—your classroom must convey the excitement and wonder of observing and learning about properties of water. Giving children multiple opportunities to explore water with a variety of interesting materials is critical. You can create a science-rich environment in your classroom by adding a second water table, or by creating water centers by making large tubs of water available on tables or the floor, so a number of children can be engaged in water exploration at any given time. Displaying interesting picture books and information books about water allows children to learn more about what they are experiencing at the water table and centers.

Organizing and placing materials for representation (such as markers, pencils, paper, and clipboards) so children have easy access to them and can return them independently will encourage ongoing representation. Charts, documentation panels, photos of children engaged in water exploration, and children's drawings of their experiences displayed at their eye level helps children build on previous explorations, while sparking new ones. Check your environment periodically to see what changes are needed to make your environment reflect the progress of the exploration. For example, are there new materials to add? Which children's work samples and documentation panels should be put away, and which should be added? Which new books reflect children's current interests about water and could enrich their experiences?

Children also need time to explore. You may need to adjust your classroom schedule so children can explore water at the water table or centers several times a week over time. Also be sure to schedule a science talk with the whole class at least once a week so children can share their observations and ideas, and learn from the experiences of others. You will also need to develop a few simple classroom rules for keeping children safe. (For more information about creating a science-rich environment, see "Getting Ready" on p. 21 and the "Classroom Environment Checklist" on p. 113.)

ENGAGE CHILDREN IN SCIENCE EXPLORATIONS

WHAT CHILDREN ARE DOING: As children move into the open exploration, some will be immediately excited by the ideas and challenges. Others will be more reluctant, perhaps playing at the water table for only a few minutes before moving on to another activity. Still others will prefer not to choose the water table or centers.

TEACHER ROLE: Spend time with those children who are ready to engage in water exploration. Do not push those who are not engaged. Some will be drawn in by your enthusiasm and the excitement of their peers. You might partner children who are excited about the exploration with children who are less engaged. For example, you might say, "Michael, can you show Ezra what you just did with the water? Onyx, could you hold that funnel for Jon?" You might also try to incorporate science into children's play. For example, you might ask children at the water table to make a lemonade machine. Try sharing some good water books as well. Reading a book might draw some children into the exploration. (See "Books and Web Sites" on p. 105.)

When children explore at the water table or center, sit with them and observe. Children who are deeply involved with their work are best left to continue to do so. You need to observe and take note. Through their actions you'll get clues about what problem they may be trying to solve and what questions they may be asking. These observations will help you guide later discussions and reflection. If children are ready to talk and listen, you might describe what children are doing and seeing. For instance, "You were able to pour water into the funnel and tube. The water really came quickly out of the bottom end of the tube!" Also encourage children to share their observations in words and actions, such as using words or pointing out with their hands where the water has been moving through tubes. Do not correct children's ideas. Rather, use words, pictures, drawings, and more direct experiences to encourage children to consider their ideas in new ways. By bringing in resources and offering new experiences, children can explore and refine their ideas. For example, looking at a book about boats might inspire children to try making boats of their own.

FOCUS AND DEEPEN CHILDREN'S EXPERIENCES AND THINKING

As children pursue their exploration of water, you will have many opportunities to push their thinking and their ideas. These opportunities will arise as children engage in conversations, as children represent and document their work, as you use resources, and as you document children's ideas and experiences.

Conversations

As children explore water, listen to their conversations with each other, and talk with them informally and during weekly discussions with a large group about their experiences, observations, and ideas.

Conversations with Other Children

WHAT CHILDREN ARE DOING: As children work side by side, their conversations with one another push them to put words to their actions and communicate some of their thinking. Their questions of one another may challenge and extend what they are doing and intrigue them with new wonderings. Their debates and arguments will push them to think more about their own ideas and those of others.

TEACHER ROLE: Children's conversations are likely to be very different from those guided by an adult. They are more likely to be more directly tied to their fantasies, rules of the game, and requests for help. Your role is to listen carefully and document what may be useful for later discussions and reflection.

Discussions with Children

WHAT CHILDREN ARE DOING: As children are engaged in their work, they may welcome interactions with the adults around them. Discussion can raise new questions and suggest new investigations, while helping them to develop their abilities to communicate about their work and thought.

TEACHER ROLE: Engaging children in conversation as they work must be done carefully and only after spending some time observing them. Children should not be interrupted unless they want to talk, and conversations should be about what they are doing and thinking. Good questions to get started include descriptive ones: "Can you tell me about what you are doing? What does the water feel like? Where did you pour the water? How did you put the funnel in the tube?" Further discussion can probe more deeply and focus on science concepts: "Where do you think the water will go when you pour it in the funnel? What do you think will happen if you put your finger over the end of the tube?"

Science Talks

WHAT CHILDREN ARE DOING: During science talks, children share their experiences and their thinking; listen to those of others; and try to make connections between what they have been doing, what others have been doing, and what they already know. It also is a time for children to struggle with new ideas and theories as old ways of understanding are challenged by new experiences.

TEACHER ROLE: Science talks are a critical part of science teaching and learning, helping children to communicate and reflect on their experiences and ideas and to focus their ideas on the science concepts and processes. Your role is to draw out children's ideas and experiences and to challenge their thinking. During your discussions, maintain a focus on the process and substance while encouraging children to tell and dramatize their stories. Use photographs of children's exploration, your notes, and books as a springboard for these discussions: "Here's a photograph of you at the water table yesterday. Can you tell us about what you were doing with that tube?" "Alexa drew this picture at the water table. Can you show us by pointing where the water went?" Further discussion can probe more deeply, helping children to compare and reflect on their observations and ideas: "Nora, the drops on your waxed paper are round, but Felicia says the drops on her waxed paper are flat. How do you think that happened?"

Discussions with a small group are easier to manage than large groups, but the science talks with a large group are important as well, so that children can hear about the ideas and experiences of many others. Begin slowly; start with five- to ten-minute science talks with a large group and increase the time as children's engagement increases. Be sure that all children who want to contribute have a chance to do so. Provide physical props to support children who are less verbal, and use your records to support those who are reluctant to speak out. For example, you might bring a baster and tubing to the meeting and say, "Nguyen, can you tell us about what you were doing with these things at the water table? Can you show us where the water went?" Such discussions may encourage children to try new things and question their thinking.

Representation and Documentation

WHAT CHILDREN ARE DOING: When children document or represent their work in various media, they think about their experiences in new ways. Using their bodies to show how water traveled through a tube or a drop slid down a windowpane can help children think more deeply about how water moves. They also reflect on their exploration when they use water play materials to demonstrate a discovery or a way they can control water flow. Some children will show interest in drawing or making a collage of some part of their exploration, but representing water movement is challenging. Photographs work well to capture water's movement. Children can even begin to decide which aspects of their exploration are important to photograph and share.

TEACHER ROLE: Documentation and children's representation can be the focus of individual or group discussions. Encourage children to demonstrate their discoveries. When you visit the water table and water center, ask children to show how they made water move, a boat sail, or drops split apart. Bring water materials to science talks so children have the option of using them to share their observations and ideas. Invite children to use their bodies to show how water moves, how objects sink in a rigid tube, or how drops move on waxed paper. Make sketches and, if possible, take photographs and video of how water is affected by children's actions and use of materials. Use your documents and children's drawings or collages to facilitate reflective conversations. "Tell us about this drawing. Where did the water travel? How did you get it to start moving? Stop moving? Why do you think you needed to use the baster?"

Using Resources

WHAT CHILDREN ARE DOING: Children learn about water through close observation in a variety of ways over long periods of time. However, direct observation is not the only way children can learn about water and its properties. They can also deepen their thinking by using books, talking with experts, and going on field trips.

TEACHER ROLE: Use resources—such as books, field trips, and guest experts—to enrich explorations of water. Be sure to display books that have engaging pictures about water's properties, so children can compare the pictures to their own observations. Field trips to a stream, a waterfall, a soda factory, and so on encourage children to compare and contrast water in these new settings to how they have experienced it in the classroom. Guest experts can provide new information about the properties of water, which can lead to new questions and investigations.

Document Children's Ideas and Experiences

WHAT CHILDREN ARE DOING: As children engage in their explorations, they are certainly thinking about many things. Their actions are the outward reflection of those thoughts. Observing and documenting what children do and say can help you understand their ideas and questions. While young children have many ideas, they tend to focus on the present. Without support, they may see experiences as somewhat isolated events and are not always aware of the development of an idea, an experience, or a project. It is also difficult for them to record and keep track of all the data they are gathering. The products of ongoing documentation can be used to provide many opportunities for children to revisit the process and progress of their work and reflect on their understanding.

TEACHER ROLE: Your role is to be the documenter. You can document children's work and the data they are gathering from their exploration in many ways—videotape and audiotape; anecdotal records; and lists of predictions, observations, and questions. You can then use this documentation to help children revisit, build on, and reflect on their data, ideas, and observations. For example, by going over your notes about children's questions, you will be able to guide them in reflecting on what they found out over time and the ideas they have developed about the properties of water. Documentation panels play a significant role in children's science explorations. It is your role to create a sequence of photos, sketches, science-related conversations, lists of predictions and observations, or children's work with brief annotations that allow children to "replay" and reflect upon what they have done and what has happened. Use the panels as a springboard for stimulating discussions, reenactments, and further explorations. (See "Guidelines for Creating Documentation Panels" on p. 115 for more information.)

Observation and Assessment

Observation, documentation, and assessment are critical steps throughout the exploration, helping you gain a picture of children's growing skills and understanding of water's properties. What children say and do will provide you with important clues about children's understanding of some of the ways water moves, some of the ways it behaves as drops and streams, how some things sink and some float in it, and how air behaves in water. What children say and do will also provide you with children's inquiry skills (such as their ability to explore, collect data, and so on), and the question they may be asking. Your analysis will help you determine the next steps to take with individual children and the group as a whole. You can also share information about children's science learning with families, your program or school, and funders.

THREE KEY ELEMENTS OF ASSESSMENT

1. Collecting data. Spend at least ten minutes three times a week collecting different kinds of data that captures children's level of engagement and their science understandings. This data can include the following:

   - Written observations that capture what children say and do and wonder about as they explore water

   - Photographs, videotapes, and audiotapes that capture children's actions and words

   - Samples of children's work that illustrate each child's growing abilities (such as observational drawings, dictated stories or poems, and two- or three-dimensional collage representations of their water experiences)

2. Analyzing data regularly. Time spent reflecting on your collection of documents will help you understand the growing skills and understandings of each child in your class. The more kinds of documents you have, the fuller picture you will have of each individual. Examine varied documents reflecting the work of each child, and look across the class to gain a picture of how the group is developing.

3. Drawing conclusions and making decisions. Analysis of the documents you have collected will help you make the important connections between your teaching and the children's learning. Use your analysis of children's growth to consider what your next steps should be with individual children and the group. Who needs encouragement in order to become fully engaged in the explorations? Who is ready for a more complex challenge? Who needs help finding a voice for their observations and ideas? This will be an ongoing process that informs your teaching, helping you refine your approach to teaching science.

A TOOL FOR SCIENCE LEARNING

"Science Outcomes: Science Inquiry Skills and Science Concepts" (pp. 120–121) will tell you what to look for as you analyze your data. This overview of learning goals is organized in two sections: science inquiry skills and science content. For each outcome, it provides three child behaviors sequenced from less to more experienced. These behaviors illustrate how a child might demonstrate her skill or understanding. Use these outcomes and behaviors to help you focus children's science learning and to assess their growth.

TOOLS FOR COLLECTING AND ORGANIZING YOUR DATA

The following three tools will help you document children's inquiry skills and growing understanding of the science concepts.

1. Observation Record. This form provides a structure and format for recording your observations of children's explorations of water and its properties. Place copies of the form strategically around the room and bring them outdoors so you can jot down your observations throughout the day. Use the observation and documentation section of each step of the teaching plan to focus on science concepts and inquiry outcomes as you complete the form. See sample form on the following page.

2. Document Annotations. Use this form to annotate photos, work samples, transcripts, or any other documents that you may have. When filling out the form, highlight what the document reveals about children's inquiry skills and their understanding of science concepts. Then attach your annotation to each document. The time you take to identify the significant science in each document will help you when it comes time to analyze children's growth and draw conclusions about your teaching. See sample on the next page.

OBSERVATION RECORD

Children's Names	Seen and Heard
Yvonne	• Tries to keep bottle full of water • Comments, "No dribbles allowed!"
Kevin	• Holds eyedropper about a foot above plate • Comments, "I'm making little ones (drops)."

DOCUMENT ANNOTATION

I made a watertable with a wall. The water was dripping down and a bubble kept coming up.

May 2001 by Autumn

Child(ren): Autumn   Date: 5/12/01

Context/Setting: Autumn was at the water table for the third day in a row. She has a grandmother in the hospital and is playing "hospital" with the tubes and syringes. She included Lloyd and Vivian in today's play.

Science Concepts Explored/Evidence: Water flows (drips) down; bubbles float up. When asked about her drawing, Autumn said, "I made a water table with a wall. The water was dripping down and a bubble kept coming up."

3. Learning Record. This record provides a format for collecting and analyzing the information you have collected about each child. Note that the content and inquiry items are the same as on the chart "Science Outcomes: Science Inquiry Skills and Science Concepts." Begin a learning record for each child as soon as you start to review your collected observations and documents. Note the evidence you have from observations, conversations, and work samples. Use dates to reference specific documents. Add to the records regularly. Your goal is to have a statement about each outcome for each child by the end of the exploration. Note where the gaps in information are and plan to focus on engaging those children. At the end of the exploration, check the appropriate box in the child growth column. See sample on the following page.

Make copies of the assessment forms that are included in the appendices and use them to document the growth of children in your classroom.

Essential Information

Most of the materials needed for *Exploring Water with Young Children* are easily accessible. The following tips can help to guide you as you look for and choose materials. While we offer suggestions for the kinds of places these materials can be found, we recommend you phone ahead to save yourself some time and possible frustration.

LEARNING RECORD

Child: <u>Hannah</u>

Science Inquiry Skills	Child Growth	Evidence
Engages, notices, wonders, questions	☐ Emerging ☐ Sometimes ☒ Consistently	9/23 Pours water into the large end of a funnel, then the small end 10/12 Attaches tubing to funnel; pours water in funnel end, then tubing end
Explores, investigates	☐ Emerging ☒ Sometimes ☐ Consistently	10/2 makes drops on plate and on wax paper; turns both over to see what happens to drops 11/10 Tests all toy trucks in classroom to see if they sink or float
Collects data	☒ Emerging ☐ Sometimes ☐ Consistently	9/30 Counts number of cups of water needed to fill different bottles 11/13 Squirts water with baster, then syringe, to see which one shoots further

---

MATERIALS

WATER TABLES

Water Tables are standard equipment in most early childhood classrooms. They often measure about 21 by 45 inches. If you do not have a water table, we recommend you borrow one for "Exploring Water." If you have trouble locating a water table for your classroom, we recommend a large (approximately 15 by 33 by 12 inches), clear plastic container to place on a tabletop or the floor, at a comfortable height for your children. If you do have a water table, borrowing a second one will allow even more children to engage in water explorations.

LARGE TUBS AND CONTAINERS

Plan to have a water center as well as a water table area open each choice time. The water center should allow room and materials for four children to explore comfortably. You might have one, two, three, or four tubs of water at the water center, depending on the size of your area and the size of available tubs. Suggestions include the following:

- Large plastic storage containers (clear ones are better, particularly for "Focused Exploration:

Sinking and Floating"). For example, clear plastic containers as small as 10 by 15 by 9 inches, up to those as large as 15 by 33 by 12 inches, are available at hardware and home supply stores.

- Shallower containers (between 6 to 9 inches deep) may be used for exploring small amounts of water. They are not recommended for sinking and floating. Containers less than 6 inches deep are of very limited value for "Exploring Water."

- Black plastic oil pans and other nonclear pans are fine for water play. They should be at least 9 inches deep to contain sufficient amounts of water, contain spills, and allow for children to explore the concepts of sink and float.

CLEAR FLEXIBLE PLASTIC TUBING

Tubing is a wonderful material to use with water and is available at most hardware stores. Tubing is sold with two dimensions: inner diameter (ID) and outside diameter (OD). The inner-diameter number will always be smaller than the outside-diameter number. A piece of tubing with an outside diameter of 5/16-inch will fit nicely into one with an inside diameter of 3/8-inch or slightly larger. The following three sizes are recommended: 3/16-inch ID and 5/16-inch OD, 3/8-inch

ID and ½-inch OD, and ½-inch ID and ⅝-inch OD so tubing of different sizes can fit snugly into each other. We advise cutting tubing into three different lengths manageable for young children—1, 2, and 3 feet long. You may find that the 3-foot lengths are difficult for children to manage at first, so you may wish to keep those out of the water table initially.

FUNNELS

Funnels move water in unique ways and come in a variety of sizes. Try to keep in mind that smaller ones (4 or 8 ounces) are generally more manageable for children. Children should be able to fit the tube of the funnel into at least one of the sizes of clear plastic tubing.

TURKEY BASTERS

These are also wonderful pumps to add to children's water exploration. They are relatively easy to find at supermarkets, hardware stores, and any store that sells kitchen supplies. The tubes of standard-size turkey basters will fit in tubing with ⅜-inch ID and larger.

WIRE WATER WALL

It is important to provide a way children can explore water flowing from above the water table. One strategy is to construct scaffolding that will sit in the water tables to hold funnels and clear tubing. A wire water wall can be made from plastic-coated closet shelving that measures at least 15 to 18 inches wide. It should be cut to a length that can fit into your water table. For a water table that measures 45 inches long, the shelving should be cut to about 38 to 40 inches. Two smaller pieces (about 12 to 15 inches) of the shelving can be used as "legs" on both ends of the wall to help keep it standing. This shelving material can be purchased from large home supply stores. The store will usually have someone available to cut it to your desired size. Cover each of the cut ends of wire with pieces of duct tape. Clothespins, C-clamps, or more duct tape can be used to attach and support the wire water wall and the pegboard to the water table.

WIRE RACKS

One way to provide children experiences moving water from one level to another at the water center is to place plastic-covered wire racks in the tubs. These racks are sold at home and hardware stores to use in kitchen cupboards for holding dishes or cans of food, and so forth.

T- AND Y-SHAPED CONNECTORS

Connected tubing gives children more opportunities to explore water flow. They are available at plumbing supply stores, hardware stores, and from companies that sell labware for science laboratories. They are sold by diameter, so they should be chosen to fit clear plastic tubing: a 5⁄16-inch T-connector will fit well in a piece of tubing with a 5⁄16-inch ID.

ADDITIONAL PUMPS

There are a variety of pumps children can use in addition to basters, and many of these other pumps move water in greater quantities.

- Recycled clear plastic pumps such as those used to dispense liquid soap are important additions to the water table.

- Bilge pumps can be purchased from marine (boating) supply stores and some hardware stores. They can move a relatively large volume of water quickly, and should initially be used with care in the classroom. They work well for emptying water tables.

- Kerosene pumps are a bit smaller, more manageable for children, and less expensive than bilge pumps. They are available at most hardware stores.

BOTTLES WITH HOLES

In "Step 3: Water in Bottles with Holes," you will be asked to provide bottles with holes for children. The holes are there to offer children opportunities to explore streams of water. Provide several clear plastic bottles or cups, each with a hole in a different location, as well as several bottles with holes in the same location. The holes can be of different sizes, so that children can compare the size of the streams of water as they come out of the holes. Clear plastic water bottles (12 to 24 ounces) that have had the top inch cut off, or large clear plastic cups can be used. Use an awl, skewer, or other sharp object to punch holes in the sides of the water bottles. You might also want to extend the size of the bottle by adding a second or even a third bottle to the first.

VELCRO PEGBOARD

In "Step 4: Water in Bottles with Holes Continues," children use a board to hold their bottles with holes so they can observe and compare streams more easily. Pegboard is one material you can use for this purpose. For a typical water table or large plastic tub, a ¼-inch-thick piece that measures 2 by 4 feet should be fine. A large plastic tub, placed on the floor next to a wall, is a good location for this setup—children will be able to place the cups more easily, and the wall will provide some support for the pegboard. Placing the pegboard in the water table off the ground will make the board difficult to reach for many children.

Velcro is a brand name for the "hook and loop" type of fastener. The rougher part is the "hook" and the fuzzier part is the "loop." For our purposes, it does not matter whether the bottles have hooks or loops attached, as long as you attach the other part to the pegboard.

Put strips of waterproof, adhesive-backed, 4-inch-wide Velcro (either hook or loop) spaced about 2 inches apart on the pegboard. Attach 1-inch-wide strips of adhesive-backed Velcro (use whatever component you did not

use on the pegboard) around clear water bottles or cups (12 to 24 ounces). Adhesive-backed, waterproof Velcro (or other brands of hook and loop fasteners) can be purchased at most hardware stores. Look for the strongest quality possible, often called "Industrial Strength."

Eyedroppers

Plastic eyedroppers can be purchased in large quantities from companies that sell school science supplies.

Clear Rigid Plastic Tubing, with End Caps

These tubes allow children to look more closely at objects sinking and floating through a couple feet of water. The tubing is generally available only through companies that specialize in manufacturing and selling plastics. It can be purchased in predetermined lengths (usually 6 feet), and cut with a hacksaw to manageable sizes. We recommend 2 feet for young children. The end caps must be snug to keep water from leaking. If

these tubes are unavailable, a tall, thin, clear plastic bottle with a lid can be substituted.

Additional Materials

Water pipe insulation can be cut to form flexible gutters, which are tied to the wire water wall.

Sample Setups to Use as Children Focus on Water Flow

Use tubs, buckets, and additional water tables to create setups that encourage children to move water from one level to another. These photos show two possible setups.

WHERE TO PURCHASE MATERIALS

WATER TABLES

Community Playthings
359 Gibson Hill Road
Chester, NY 10918-2321
800-777-4244
www.communityplaythings.com

Lakeshore Learning Materials
2695 East Dominguez Street
P.O. Box 6261
Carson, CA 90749
800-421-5354
www.lakeshorelearning.com

T- AND Y-SHAPED CONNECTORS

- Local plumbing supply and hardware stores

Carolina Biological Supply Company
2700 York Road
Burlington, NC 27215
800-334-5551
www.carolina.com

In the Carolina catalog they are referred to as
Y-Shaped Propylene Connecting Tubes
(RG-71-1833 is one of the sizes).

EYEDROPPERS

Learning Things, Inc.
4381 34th St. S.
St. Petersburg, FL 33711
800-284-5688
www.learningthings.us

RIGID PLASTIC TUBING

AIN Plastics (a ThyssenKrupp Materials Company)
P.O. Box 151
Mount Vernon, NY 10550
800-431-2451
www.ainplastics.com

We use Cellulose Acetate Butyrate (CAB) tubing
Size number: 18B (ID=1⅛-inch, OD=1¼-inch)
End cap stock number: 289 (ID=1¼-inch)
The tubing comes in 6-foot lengths, and can be cut
easily into 2-foot pieces with a hacksaw.

Involving Families

A number of children's family members are likely to
have knowledge or abilities that will be valuable as
you engage in exploring water. Some may know about
boats and how they are made; some may be plumbers.
Find out which resources exist in your community of
families, and try to make use of some family members.
These visits enhance both children's learning and the
home-to-school connection.

It will be helpful to set the stage for family support
early. At the beginning of the exploration, send home
the letter to families (p. 106) with each child to introduce families to the exploration. Let them know what
children will do and learn, and suggest ways that they
can support their children's science learning.

You can also extend children's science learning by
suggesting science-related activities for families to do
at home and in the community. These activities can
reinforce the science children are learning in the classroom and outdoors, while helping children and families see science phenomena in their daily lives. As the
exploration progresses, send home "Families Exploring
Water" (p. 107), which offers water activities that
caregivers can do with their children.

Books and Web Sites

It is important to evaluate books as well as any other
water resources that you select for children to use in
the classroom. Select carefully, because the materials
that you choose will be valuable resources for the children's explorations. It is important that all resources
meet these basic criteria:

- Characters and content should reflect cultural di-
  versity. Not every book must represent different
  cultures, but your collection should as a whole.

- Stereotypes should be absent.

- Content should be scientifically accurate.

The list of resources for children is broken into additional subdivisions. Each category contains selection
criteria and a set of annotated examples to help you
identify high-quality resources. But keep in mind that
books go out of print and are not always available. If
the examples listed below are not obtainable, use the

Dear Families,

You may have noticed that your children are naturally curious about the world around them. They may be especially excited and interested in water, one of the most common elements in our world. Water not only offers rich opportunities for exploration, it is also a part of children's everyday experiences, whether they are taking a bath, watching rain as it drips down a window-pane, or playing at the water table.

As part of our science curriculum this year we are going to investigate water. Your children will develop a scientific approach to their investigation of water as part of small group water activities inside at the water table and outdoors (when weather permits). Through their water play, children will learn about important science ideas as they explore the properties of water and investigate how water moves.

At school, your children will do the following:

- Pour, scoop, and squirt with various cups, bottles, basters, and eyedroppers
- Move water up and down using clear plastic tubes and funnels
- Examine drops of water
- Explore what sinks and floats
- Draw and paint pictures that show their ideas about water
- Share their thinking and ideas

Rest assured that we have very clear rules to ensure children's safety. Although we provide smocks for children to wear as they explore water, please send an extra set of clothes for your child so that if he does get wet, we can help him change into dry clothes as soon as possible.

You can really help with our water exploration by encouraging children to explore water at home. Children will delight in exploring how water moves while in the bath or shower. And their experiences will be enriched when you provide plastic cups and empty shampoo bottles, so they can experiment with using different types of materials to move and control water. You can also help by thinking more about water yourself and by inviting your children to think about these questions with you. For example, you might think about how many ways you use water, where water comes from, and where water can be seen flowing or dripping. These discussions will promote your child's curiosity and interest, while also helping children to think about water as a valuable natural resource.

We can also use your assistance and expertise at school. If you have time to volunteer, come help us as we explore. An extra pair of hands is always welcome. Or if you are knowledgeable about plumbing or anything else related to our study of water, let us know. We'd love to have you share your experience with all the children.

Water is wonderful! Dive into our study with us!

---

given criteria to choose others like them. It is best to have different kinds of books and resources available for children to use, and remember that types of books can overlap.

There is also a list of resource books and Web sites for teachers that you may find helpful in gathering information about water and photos to use in the classroom. Specific Web sites may change; those listed are examples of the kinds of sites that can support the exploration.

BOOKS FOR CHILDREN

NONFICTION

Listed below are three different kinds of nonfiction books for children: image books, information books, and biographies. Each of these nonfiction books has at least three criteria in common—scientifically accurate content; detailed illustrations or photographs that give children information and stimulate ideas; and content that is inherently interesting to children, stimulates their exploration, and raises questions for them.

FAMILIES EXPLORING WATER

You and your child are around water all the time: in the kitchen, in the bathroom, at the beach, or in the rain. All of these experiences can present opportunities to explore water together. What's most important is to try to maintain a positive attitude about water exploration, even when there is a strong possibility that water will make some things (and people) wet. By exploring water together, you and your child will learn more about each other and the properties of water.

Tips for Indoor Water Explorations

Children will delight in exploring the properties of water and how it moves while in the bath or at the kitchen sink. And you can enrich children's experiences when you provide some of the following materials:

- Different sizes and shapes of clear plastic containers to invite filling and emptying
- Empty shampoo bottles with small openings to help children focus on squirting and the drops themselves
- Turkey basters and empty plastic liquid soap bottles with pumps so children can explore ways to move water
- Objects of different shapes so children can explore what sinks and floats
- Clear plastic flexible tubes to encourage children's investigation of water flow

While at the kitchen sink or in the bathtub, encourage children to experiment to see how they can do the following:

- Use the materials to make the water move in different directions (up and down)
- Make the water go at different speeds (slow and fast)
- Explore which objects sink and which float
- Create bubbles
- Make a drop come out of the faucet
- Turn their water flow back into a drip

Tips for Outdoor Water Explorations

You can also extend your child's investigations of water to the outdoors by taking a rainy-day walk. As you walk together, encourage your child to explore and notice the following:

- How puddles form on different surfaces (grass, sidewalks, leaves) and then disappear
- How drops drip down windowpanes or off of cars
- How water flows off roofs, leaves, tree branches, and umbrellas; water races down gutters, gullies, and streams
- How children can make some of the water stop flowing or change its direction

Tips for Water Talks

As your child explores the properties of water, how it moves, and how air behaves in it, use these tips to get the water talks flowing:

- Talk with your child about how she uses the materials. ("The funnel is really helping you get water into that bottle!")
- Ask open-ended questions. ("How did you get the water to move? How did you get the water flow to stop? How did you get the water to flow fast? Slow?")
- Describe what your child does to move water or make it stop. ("Wow! You made the water gush really fast.")
- Wonder out loud with children. ("I wonder what would happen to that bubble if you turned that tubing upside down?")

Provide your child with the support she needs to share her thinking:

- Give your child time to think before she responds to your questions and comments. Silent time is okay.
- Find ways for your child to show you what she knows (for example, using the pump to show you how she can make water move up or down).

Avoid comments that could limit your child's thinking. Avoid the following:

- Explaining the science
- Correcting ideas (rather, ask more questions)
- Moving on too quickly (allow the child to decide when to move on)

Image Books

Image books for children ages three through five are any books that use large, detailed illustrations or photographs to convey information and inspire children to explore further. These can include books that are specifically written for children or books that are meant for adults or older children but have engaging pictures that inform and stimulate young children's thinking.

Examples of image books include the following:

- Asch, Frank. 2000. *Water*. New York: Voyager.

  This basic introduction to water is enriched by the beautiful watercolor illustrations that will captivate any child's attention. The bright images, serving as representations of water, are paired with simple words. Young children are sure to remember the illustrations in this book as they begin to develop their appreciation for water.

- Kerley, Barbara. 2002. *A Cool Drink of Water*. Washington, D.C.: National Geographic Society.

  These photographs from all over the world illustrate some of the many ways people store and drink water. The text is simple, but the pictures will be the source of any number of conversations about cultures and water.

- Wick, Walter. 1997. *A Drop of Water*. New York: Scholastic Press.

  This book with photographs of water is a must-have for any classroom. The photographs are incredibly beautiful and are sure to stimulate children's questions about and interest in water. The book's striking photographs of water droplets, snowflakes, and water in other states are the highlight and will capture the attention of all children. *A Drop of Water* is also a valuable resource for teachers.

Information Books

Information books for children ages three through five are books that focus on specific topics, such as waterfalls, fountains, or sinking and floating. Or they can be books that focus on specific questions, such as how a boat floats or what a snowflake looks like. These books provide children with information that answers questions and raises more questions.

Examples of information books include the following:

- Bradley, Kimberly Brubaker, photographs by Margaret Miller. 2001. *Pop! A Book about Bubbles*. New York: HarperCollins Publishers.

  Everyone loves bubbles. The beautiful photographs illustrate bubbles, and the language describes bubbles in a number of contexts, including soap bubbles as well as bubbles in milk, soda, and water.

- Cobb, Vicki. 2002. *I Get Wet*. New York: HarperCollins Publishers.

  This is one of the titles in the Vicki Cobb Science Play Series. The intriguing illustrations, simple language, and shape of the text are an open invitation for the reader (and friends) to find some water and explore.

- Simon, Seymour, and Nicole Fauteux. 2003. *Let's Try It Out in the Water*. New York: Aladdin Paperbacks.

  The prolific children's science author Seymour Simon engages young children with his Let's Try It Out series. This book encourages hands-on water exploration with provocative questions and the frequent suggestion: "Let's try it out."

Biographies

Biographies for children ages three through five are real stories about real people. Biographical characters should be related to the topic of study, and the story should be focused and comprehensible enough for children of this age.

An example of a biography follows:

- Martin, Jacqueline Briggs. 1998. *Snowflake Bentley*. New York: Houghton Mifflin.

  Winner of the Caldecott Medal, this book tells the story of Wilson Bentley, a man who was fascinated by snowflakes. He spent much of his life taking photographs of snowflakes, examining the tiny crystals and the structure of each flake. In addition to the story, there are sidebars that provide factual details. The illustrations, which are hand-colored woodcuts, are sure to draw children in to the wonder and delight felt by Bentley himself.

FICTION

Listed below are two different kinds of fiction books for children: fact and fantasy and real-life fiction. Each of these fiction books has at least three of the following criteria in common—developmentally appropriate presentation (rhythm, repetition, story length, vocabulary, font size); content that is inherently interesting to children, stimulates their exploration, and raises questions for them; illustrations that explain the story; and a substantial amount of scientifically accurate content.

FACT AND FANTASY

A major feature of fact and fantasy books for children ages three through five is that they should raise questions for children about scientific phenomena and spark their interests. Books that view the natural world through the eyes of different cultures can help children begin to understand science from different perspectives. While much of the content should be scientifically accurate, these books may also contain some fantasy.

Examples of fact and fantasy books for children include the following:

- Allen, Pamela. 1996. *Who Sank the Boat?* New York: Paper Star.

  This is the story of some animal friends who one day decide to go for a row in the bay. As each animal gets on the boat, it sinks lower and lower in the water. Children will want to revisit the story again and again to see who sank the boat. The story is sure to get them thinking about sinking and floating.

- Brown, Stephanie Gwyn. 2003. *Professor Aesop's The Crow and the Pitcher.* Berkeley: Tricycle Press.

  This is a science based interpretation of one of Aesop's fables. The story highlights properties of water and the skills and dispositions required by a crow determined to drink water that is at the bottom of a deep, narrow pitcher. Colorful drawings and simple text draw children into the crow's predicament. This book will encourage children to explore water displacement.

REAL-LIFE FICTION

These books differ from other fiction books because, while the story is fictional, the science content is accurate. Where other fiction books might contain bits of fantasy, these do not. Similar to fact and fantasy books, real-life fiction books should also raise questions for children about scientific phenomena.

Examples of real-life fiction books for children include the following:

- Locker, Thomas. 1997. *Water Dance.* San Diego: Voyager Books.

  Water Dance is a book that combines art and science. Each page is a beautifully illustrated natural scene in which water plays a major role (a river, a waterfall, and so on). The text that accompanies each scene is more a description, or even a poem, than a story. The final three pages of the book tell the more scientific story of the water cycle.

- Yolen, Jane, and Barbara Cooney. 1995. *Letting Swift River Go.* Boston: Little Brown & Company.

  Written for children slightly older than preschool age, this is based on the story of how the Quabbin Reservoir in Massachusetts was formed, as seen through the eyes of a child. The reader will learn of preparations people made to move their homes and lives before the valley is flooded, as well as hear of some of the smaller details that are of concern to the young narrator.

POETRY

Poetry for children ages three through five encompasses characteristics of both fiction and nonfiction books. It can be either completely scientifically accurate or contain bits of fantasy and should contain content that is inherently interesting to children, stimulates their exploration, and raises questions for them. Unlike other books for children, however, poetry uses words rather than pictures to illustrate experiences and phenomena, often containing rhyming verses. This does not mean that these books will have no pictures, just that the words will be able to draw a picture themselves.

Examples of poetry books include the following:

- Cunningham, David. 1996. *A Crow's Journey.* Morton Grove, Ill.: Albert Whitman & Co.

  A crow follows melting snow as it finds a mountain stream, then a river, and eventually, the sea. The rhyming language is simple; the realistic illustrations, including a number of images of water, are beautiful.

- Levy, Constance. 2002. *Splash! Poems of Our Watery World.* New York: Orchard Books.

  Although written with slightly older children in mind, the poems in this book deal with phenomena young children experience all the time, as indicated by titles like "Drops," "Pour," and "Soap Bubbles." Much of the language is accessible to

three- through five-year-olds: "The river over-
flowed its banks / and all that I could see / were
bright green tops / of flooded trees / poking up /
like broccoli."

RESOURCE BOOKS AND WEB SITES FOR TEACHERS

These resources should be used only by the teacher to
gather information, get ideas to use in the classroom,
or find photographs of waterfalls, rivers, and the like.
The main criterion for these resources is that they
should include scientifically accurate content. Although young children will not use the books, it may
be helpful if they are written simply and clearly so
teachers can access information without wading
through difficult scientific language. Also be aware
that any Web sites listed here might be discontinued.
They are listed as examples of the kinds of information available on the Web.

RESOURCE BOOKS

- Education Development Center, Inc. 2003.
  Liquids (a module from Insights: An Elementary
  Hands-On Inquiry Science Curriculum).
  Dubuque, Iowa: Kendall Hunt Publishing Co.

  This teacher guide is intended for use at grades
  two and three. While it includes activities that
  you would not take directly to the classroom,
  it is useful for teachers as a resource on the science involved in water.

- National Science Resources Center. 1997. *Solids
  and Liquids* (a module from Science and Technology for Children). Burlington, N.C.: Carolina
  Biological Supply Co.

  This teacher guide is intended for grade 1.

- Wick, Walter. 1997. *A Drop of Water.* New York:
  Scholastic Press.

  This book with photographs of water is a must-
  have for any classroom. The photographs are
  beautiful and are sure to stimulate children's questions about and interest in water. The book also
  provides information, but its striking photographs of water droplets, snowflakes, and water in
  other states are the highlight—certain to capture
  the attention of all children.

WEB SITES

- *www.dramainnature.com/photographs_of
  _waterfalls.htm*

  This site has some beautiful and unusual photographs of waterfalls. Children may be interested
  in seeing the different types of waterfalls—those
  that appear to be one stream and those that are
  wider and have many streams. These photographs can also be printed out to display around
  your classroom. They will look especially inviting
  if you have access to a color printer. This is one
  of many sites on the Web that has pictures of
  waterfalls.

- *www.esiponline.org*

  The Elementary Science Integration Projects
  (ESIP) provide a number of resources about the
  use of children's books in science. Though aimed
  at elementary teachers, this site has much appli-
  cation for preschool teachers. Through this site
  you can subscribe to Search It Science, a search
  engine for putting you in touch with more than
  4,500 children's science books.

- *www.freefoto.com/pictures/nature/fountain/index.asp*

  This site has many photographs of fountains in
  various amounts of detail. In some photographs,
  the fountains look like large clumps of water,
  while in others you can see the smaller streams
  and droplets of water. Children may enjoy looking at these pictures with you and noticing the
  details in the fountains.

- *www.nesc.wvu.edu/ndwc/ndwc_kids_dwinfo.htm*

  The National Drinking Water Clearinghouse
  seeks to provide information and resources that
  relate to water. This particular site, Drinking
  Water Kids, offers resources (children's books,
  curriculum materials, Web sites, and so on) aimed
  specifically at teaching children about water.

appendices

Children's Representations of Water

As one way of helping three-, four-, and five-year-olds develop understandings about properties of water, the *Exploring Water with Young Children* teacher's guide suggests young children represent some of their experiences. But it is difficult to represent water, whether it's swirling through a funnel, being absorbed by a paper towel, or buoying a boat. Because it is so difficult to capture moving water in two- or three-dimensional representation, children who draw or model a piece of their exploration tend to represent the materials they used, and not the water.

Representing an experience with water is valuable when it helps children reflect on their observations and ideas about the properties of water. For some children, this may mean drawing or fashioning collage materials to represent the water materials and then adding lines or materials to represent water. Other children might need you to draw or cut out shapes of the materials so they can concentrate on adding lines or pieces of paper, ribbon, or yarn to represent water.

The following are suggestions for helping children represent their observations and experiences that are likely to encourage reflection. Children will reflect on their experiences as they represent them and when you refer to their representations during subsequent days' explorations, as well as during science talks and other reflective conversations.

REPRESENTING MOVING WATER

When children are using flexible tubing, try the following:

- Invite children to use their fingers to show you the path the water took as they moved it.
- Sketch on a whiteboard or chart paper materials children are using and then invite them to use a blue marker to draw the path the water took.
- Encourage children to use collage materials to represent the water materials they've been using, and then add blue string, ribbon, or marker to represent the path the water took.

When children are using bottles with holes, try the following:

- Involve children in using their fingers to trace in the air the shape of a stream they just made.
- Sketch the bottles with holes on a whiteboard or chart paper, and invite children to use a marker to add to your sketch by drawing the streams they have been making and observing.
- Use Styrofoam cups to represent the bottles with holes children are using to create streams; poke holes in each cup to correspond to the holes in the bottles; provide pipe cleaners or flexible craft wire children use to represent the shape of the

streams; suggest they stick the wire "streams" into the holes in their Styrofoam cup.

- Provide clipboards, paper, and markers so children can draw the bottles with holes, and the streams they are making.

REPRESENTING DROPS

As you visit the water center, invite children to do the following:

- Make their body take the shape of a drop on waxed paper, or a paper plate.

- Make the sound a drop makes as it hits waxed paper, or a paper towel.

- Use a clipboard and marker to draw the shape of the drops they are making, top view and side view.

- Use clay or plasticine to make the shapes of the drops they are making.

REPRESENTING SINKING AND FLOATING

As you visit the water center or water table, try the following:

- Encourage children to move their hands through the air to show how a particular object moves as it sinks (or floats up in a rigid tube).

- Hand out clipboards, paper, and markers so children can draw the tub of water and a floating object; encourage them to look at the clear tub from the side and to draw a line through the object to represent the water level.

- Hand out clipboards, paper, and markers so children can sketch a boat they built and have just sailed, including a line to show where the boat sits in the water.

- Set up an easel and paints at the water center so children can paint a picture of the tub of water with a few objects in it.

- Bring the tub of water, including the sinking and floating objects, to the art table; provide collage materials so children can make collages of the tub of water with a few objects sinking and floating in it.

USING PHOTOGRAPHS

Photographs can also help children reflect on their experiences with water—they help children remember what they did and what they saw. Keep in mind that some photographs can be more effective than others. Images that show water moving, the shape of a drop or stream, or the position of an object floating in water all help children reflect on the properties of water. Children can be involved in choosing which images should be photographed. Help them develop the ability to recognize interesting photo opportunities by talking about the ones you see. For example, you might say the following:

- *Look at the way the water is sticking to the side of the tube as it moves from the funnel to this bucket. I'm going to take a picture of that.*

- *I just saw that stream turn into drops. Can you make that happen again so I can take a picture of the moment the stream changes into drops?*

Photographs also need to be large enough for children to see the water, whether it be a drop, a stream, or a flow from a large funnel. Digital photos are nice because they can be printed on letter-size paper, and they are so immediate. If you use 35 mm film, try to get your photographs developed as quickly as possible, and use a photocopier's zoom feature to make 8 by 10-inch enlargements. Black and white copies are fine.

DEMONSTRATIONS

When children demonstrate something they did during a water exploration, they deepen their understandings of the properties of water—they are required to revisit the experience, organize their thoughts, and communicate their observations. You can encourage children to demonstrate something they noticed or discovered about water by visiting the water table and water center during choice time and asking them to repeat something they just did. Perhaps they'll show you the way they made drops come together on waxed paper, changed the shape of a ball of plasticine so it would float, or emptied a bucket of water using a baster connected to tubing. You can also encourage children to demonstrate their experiences, observations, or discoveries during science talks by providing a bucket of materials for them to use as props, without water. In both cases, you can ask children to share the ways they were able to make water behave in certain ways, and probe their thinking about why what they do makes water move in particular ways.

CLASSROOM ENVIRONMENT CHECKLIST

Classroom Materials Inventory

Complete an inventory of the materials you have for the "Exploring Water" exploration by filling in the middle column of the chart below. In the right column, list what you need to obtain. Refer to p. 102 for a more complete list of recommended materials.

Item	Inventory	Needs
Water table (21" x 45")		
Large plastic tubs		
Long-sleeved water smocks		
Clear plastic containers in a variety of shapes and sizes		
Turkey basters		
Clear flexible tubing (three sizes)		
Clear plastic funnels (three sizes)		
T- and Y- tube connectors (three sizes)		
Wire water wall (plastic-coated closet shelving)		
Pegboard		
Velcro		
Clear plastic cups or bottles with holes		
Eyedroppers		
Surfaces on which to explore drops: rigid plastic plates, waxed paper, aluminum foil, fabric scraps		
Clear plastic containers, at least 8" deep		
Sink and float objects		
Clear plastic rigid tubes, end caps		
Materials for making boats: Styrofoam trays, aluminum foil, wood, cardboard, masking tape		

Set Up the Classroom

Complete the chart below to help you plan how your space will reflect your study of water. Use the check column on the right to note your accomplishments. See p. 18 for specific recommendations.

Recommendations	Plans	✔
Water table area that accommodates four or more children		
Water center area to accommodate four or more children		
Wall space		
Book space		
Accessible water materials		
Storage for clean-up materials such as sponges, towels, and a mop		
Storage for wet smocks and extra dry clothes		

Plan the Schedule

Two special times for inquiry are recommended on p. 22: choice time and science talk. Use the following chart to assess your needs and plan necessary changes to your daily schedule.

Time	Current Schedule	Change in Schedule
Choice time 45–60 minutes of choice time at least three times per week		
Science talk 10–15 minutes as a whole group at least once per week		

GUIDELINES FOR CREATING DOCUMENTATION PANELS

How Do I Make a Documentation Panel?

1. Collect documents.

- Collect related work samples—collages, drawings, photographs of children using movement to describe water.

- Collect dialogue. Record science-related conversations with and among children, jot down a conversation that can be typed up later, or ask children to tell you about their work or a photo.

- Pull together notes and data that have been collected during the exploration—science inquiry charts, a list of predictions, descriptive observations, new questions, and so on.

- If you have access to a camera, take photos of children using materials to make drops, streams, and to control water flow. Or photograph them observing the results of their sink and float tests or the ways drops move on different surfaces. Capture images of children in the act of moving, controlling, or observing water. Enlarge 3 by 5-inch and 4 by 6-inch photos on a photocopier, or print digital photos on letter-size paper (the photos should be large enough for a group of children to view together).

2. Decide the panel's focus.

- Discovery—Children discover bubbles in their rigid tubes.

- Exploration—Children explore, asking "What rises in water? What sinks?"

- Data collection—Children measure how high a baster can squirt water, or they sequence containers by volume—from which holds the least water to which holds the most.

- Comparison—Children compare and contrast their local fountain to the streams they make using bottles with holes.

- Tool use—Children use hand lenses to look more closely at drops and pumps to move water through tubing.

How Do I Put Together the Panel?

1. Arrange your documents in chronological order, from left to right, across the board in a single, straight line. Adhere your photos with a glue stick, rubber cement, or two-sided tape. (White glue wrinkles paper.)

2. Add text to your panel. Suggestions include the following:

- Interview the children whose work is featured on the panel and use some of their words as captions under their work samples.

- Add the question or challenge that guided the children's focused exploration.

3. Add a title that focuses your reading audience on the panel's key message. For example:

- Max decides which material would make the best raincoat.

- Making a juice machine.

How Can I Display the Panels and Share Them with Families?

- Post the panels at children's eye level. When you run out of wall space, move the ones that aren't currently being used into the hall or to some other location where families and colleagues might enjoy them.

- Invite children to share panels with family members. Post a couple of questions next to the panel to prompt conversation and help focus it on the aspect of science inquiry featured on the panel.

- Share panels during parent conferences. Use them to reflect on specific aspects of children's science experiences and their growth and development.

Observation Record

Teacher_____ Date: _____

Setting:_____

Check one: ☐ Open Exploration   ☐ Focused Exploration

Check one: ☐ Flow   ☐ Streams   ☐ Drops   ☐ Sink and float

Step: _____

Children's Names	Seen and Heard

DOCUMENT ANNOTATION

Child(ren): _____ Date: _____

Context/Setting:_____

_____

_____

Science Concepts Explored/Evidence: _____

_____

_____

DOCUMENT ANNOTATION

Child(ren): _____ Date: _____

Context/Setting:_____

_____

_____

Science Concepts Explored/Evidence: _____

_____

_____

DOCUMENT ANNOTATION

Child(ren): _____ Date: _____

Context/Setting:_____

_____

_____

Science Concepts Explored/Evidence: _____

_____

_____

Learning Record: Part I

Child _____ Birth Date: _____

Date Exploration Began: _____ Completed: _____

Science Inquiry Skills	Child Growth	Evidence
Engages, notices, wonders, questions	☐ Emerging ☐ Sometimes ☐ Consistently	
Begins to explore, investigate	☐ Emerging ☐ Sometimes ☐ Consistently	
Collects data	☐ Emerging ☐ Sometimes ☐ Consistently	
Records and represents experience	☐ Emerging ☐ Sometimes ☐ Consistently	
Reflects on experience	☐ Emerging ☐ Sometimes ☐ Consistently	
Uses language to communicate feelings	☐ Emerging ☐ Sometimes ☐ Consistently	
Shares, discusses, and reflects with group	☐ Emerging ☐ Sometimes ☐ Consistently	

LEARNING RECORD: PART II

Child _____ Birth Date: _____

Date Exploration Began: _____ Completed: _____

Science Concepts	Child Growth	Evidence
Water flows down, unless acted upon	☐ Emerging ☐ Sometimes ☐ Consistently	
Water takes the shape of its container	☐ Emerging ☐ Sometimes ☐ Consistently	
Water sticks to itself	☐ Emerging ☐ Sometimes ☐ Consistently	
Water sticks to other materials	☐ Emerging ☐ Sometimes ☐ Consistently	
Air makes bubbles in water and rises to the surface	☐ Emerging ☐ Sometimes ☐ Consistently	
Some things sink in water, and others float	☐ Emerging ☐ Sometimes ☐ Consistently	

OUTCOMES CHARTS

The two outcomes charts that follow will help you to describe and record your children's progress. You may also find them useful when talking with others about the goals of *Exploring Water with Young Children*. The first chart, "Science Outcomes," is in two parts: science inquiry skills and science concepts. Each skill or concept is defined in the column on the left. On the right are three levels of behaviors, starting with simple and moving to more complex. What your children will achieve will depend on their level of maturity and prior experiences.

The second chart is "Connections between Inquiry Skills and Outcomes in Other Domains." This chart provides a visual presentation of how science inquiry skills relate to outcomes or skills in other areas. The inquiry skills are listed in the left-hand column. Language, literacy, and mathematics skills, as well as social abilities and approach to learning, appear at the top. Checked boxes show where inquiry skills support abilities in other areas. While the outcomes of other subject areas listed are based on the Head Start Child Outcomes Framework, they are also relevant to a range of early childhood programs.

SCIENCE OUTCOMES: SCIENCE INQUIRY SKILLS AND SCIENCE CONCEPTS

Science Inquiry Skills	Water Exploration Behaviors
Engages, notices, wonders, questions: Engages in open-ended explorations of water with different materials; forms questions that guide actions.	• Tries to explore water; willingly goes to water table or other water centers. • Persists in exploring water (such as tries to learn more about water by using materials in different ways). • Tries a variety of water play setups with a variety of materials.
Begins to explore, investigate: Engages in simple investigations to extend observations, test predictions, and pursue questions.	• Explores water and materials as if asking "What will happen if I try *this*?" • Tries to find ways to answer specific questions. ("Can I squirt water with the eyedropper like I did with the baster?") • Designs simple investigations. ("I'm going to try to put tubing on the end of the baster to see if I can make a longer baster.")
Collects data: Uses senses, varied tools, and simple measures to gather data.	• Uses sight and touch when gathering information about water. • Attempts basic measurement (such as compares how much water is in various containers); uses nonstandard comparison. ("The water is taller so there's more!") • Uses materials and containers based on how they can best be used (such as is comfortable using a baster or funnel properly).
Records and represents experience: Describes and records experiences and information through a variety of means, including two- and three-dimensional representation, charts, and movement.	• Attempts simple line drawings of water materials. • Creates two- and three-dimensional representations of water materials that incorporate several characteristics. • Begins to focus on the movement of water in their representations (such as using arrows to indicate direction of flow).
Reflects on experiences: Explores patterns and relationships among experiences; makes reasonable predictions, explanations, and generalizations based on experience.	• Draws on prior experiences when describing, comparing, and talking about water. ("I play with water in the bath.") • Bases predictions and explanations on observations and data from past experiences. ("If you squeeze it, the water's gonna squirt!") • Connects observations and data from multiple explorations, identifying patterns and relationships and stating conclusions. (Every time the water gets in, the boat sinks.)
Uses language to communicate findings: Develops increased vocabulary and ability to communicate observations and ideas.	• Responds to direct questions about characteristics of water and materials. • Contributes more detailed descriptions and ideas about their water experiences. • Mentions various characteristics of different materials and explains why they were used when they were.
Shares, discusses, and reflects with group: Shares materials, tasks, and ideas; collaborates in joint investigations.	• Explores water alone or alongside others. • Explores water with a small group. • Plans, negotiates, and discusses water in a small group.

SCIENCE OUTCOMES: SCIENCE INQUIRY SKILLS AND SCIENCE CONCEPTS (CONT'D)

Science Concepts	Water Exploration Behaviors
Water moves in particular ways: Shows increasing awareness of how water moves or flows. Shows increasing awareness that water usually flows down, but that in certain circumstances it can be made to move up or sideways (such as when using basters or pumps).	• Anticipates water will usually move down and is easy to spill. • Shows awareness that water can move through a number of materials, including thin and thick tubing and funnels. • Recognizes that water can be made to move up or sideways when force is exerted on it (such as by squeezing or with a pump). Recognizes that drops have some of the same characteristics as larger amounts of water (such as usually moves down unless squirted from an eyedropper).
Water takes the shape of its container: Shows increasing awareness that water will look different in different containers.	• Notices that water must be contained (such as child pours water repeatedly from one container to another). • Begins to notice that all kinds of containers can be used with water (such as bottles, caps, and tubing). • Begins to show awareness that containers with holes can hold water for a short while, depending on the size and location of the holes.
Properties of water—adhesion and cohesion: Shows increasing awareness that water can appear in small quantities such as small streams and drops (cohesion) and appears different on different surfaces (adhesion).	• Begins to show awareness that water has a number of different properties (such as that it overflows containers, spills, drips, and splashes). • Begins to notice that drops of water of any size seem to keep a rounded shape, and that they usually return to this shape as they are pushed and dragged along certain surfaces. • Becomes more careful in making drops of varying sizes and in observing how drops appear in different circumstances (such as tries to make very small drops, notices different shapes on different surfaces).
Objects can sink, float, or stay suspended in water: Becomes aware that when placed in water, some things remain on the surface (float), and others go under the surface to either sink to the bottom or to stay suspended. Aware that floating and sinking objects have certain characteristics. (Note: The goal is to make predictions, not for children to understand density, which is a more difficult concept.)	• Begins to notice that some of the objects played with in the water table float and others sink. • Begins to notice that materials that sink or float usually remain sinking or floating even if left in water. • Shows awareness that objects that sink or float will usually do the same thing every time they are placed in water.
Air takes up space and floats to the top of water: Shows increasing awareness that bubbles can be seen in certain circumstances, and that air can move water.	• Begins to notice bubbles in water when pouring, or using a baster or pump. • Begins to notice that bubbles seem to appear consistently and can often be predicted. • Shows awareness that water can often fill "empty" spaces, but in some situations it cannot.

CONNECTIONS BETWEEN INQUIRY SKILLS AND OUTCOMES IN OTHER DOMAINS

LANGUAGE ➡ *and* **SCIENCE** ⬇	Shows progress in understanding and following simple and multistep directions.	Shows increasing abilities to understand and use language to communicate information, experience, ideas, feelings, opinions, questions, and so on.	Progresses in abilities to initiate and respond appropriately in conversation and discussions with peers and adults.	Links new learning experiences and vocabulary to what is already known about a topic.
Explores/questions—Engages in open-ended explorations; forms questions that guide actions.		✓	✓	
Begins to investigate—Engages in simple investigations to extend observations, test predictions, and pursue questions.	✓	✓	✓	✓
Collects data—Uses senses, varied tools, and simple measures to gather data.	✓	✓		
Records and represents experience—Describes and records experiences and information through a variety of means, including two- and three-dimensional representation, charts, and movement.		✓		✓
Synthesizes and analyzes data from experiences—Sees patterns in data and relationships among experiences; makes reasonable predictions, explanations, and generalizations based on experience.		✓	✓	✓
Uses language to communicate findings—Develops increased vocabulary and ability to communicate observations and ideas.		✓	✓	✓
Collaborates—Shares materials, tasks, and ideas; collaborates in joint investigations.		✓	✓	

CONNECTIONS BETWEEN INQUIRY SKILLS AND OUTCOMES IN OTHER DOMAINS (CONT'D)

LITERACY and **SCIENCE**	Progresses in abilities to retell and dictate stories from books or experiences, act out stories in dramatic play, and predict what will happen next in a story.	Develops an understanding that writing is a way of communicating for a variety of purposes.	Begins to represent stories and experiences through pictures, dictation, and play.	Experiments with a growing variety of writing tools, such as pencils, crayons, and computers.
Explores/questions—Engages in open-ended explorations; forms questions that guide actions.				
Begins to investigate—Engages in simple investigations to extend observations, test predictions, and pursue questions.	✓			
Collects data—Uses senses, varied tools, and simple measures to gather data.		✓		✓
Records and represents experience—Describes and records experiences and information through a variety of means, including two- and three-dimensional representation, charts, and movement.	✓	✓	✓	✓
Synthesizes and analyzes data from experiences—Sees patterns in data and relationships among experiences; makes reasonable predictions, explanations, and generalizations based on experience.	✓	✓	✓	✓
Uses language to communicate findings—Develops increased vocabulary and ability to communicate observations and ideas.	✓	✓	✓	✓
Collaborates—Shares materials, tasks, and ideas; collaborates in joint investigations.				

CONNECTIONS BETWEEN INQUIRY SKILLS AND OUTCOMES IN OTHER DOMAINS (CONT'D)

MATHEMATICS and SCIENCE	Begins to recognize, describe, compare, and name common shapes and their parts and attributes.	Increases understanding of directionality, order, positions of objects, and words (*up, down, over, under, top, bottom,* and so on).	Enhances abilities to recognize, duplicate, and extend simple patterns using a variety of materials.	Increases abilities to match, sort, put in a series, regroup, and compare objects according to one or two attributes (such as shape or size).	Shows progress in using standard and nonstandard measures for length and area of objects.	Participates in creating and using real and pictorial graphs.
Explores/questions—Engages in open-ended explorations; forms questions that guide actions.						
Begins to investigate—Engages in simple investigations to extend observations, test predictions, and pursue questions.				✓	✓	✓
Collects data—Uses senses, varied tools, and simple measures to gather data.	✓	✓		✓	✓	✓
Records and represents experience—Describes and records experiences and information through a variety of means, including two- and three-dimensional representation, charts, and movement.	✓	✓		✓	✓	✓
Synthesizes and analyzes data from experiences—Sees patterns in data and relationships among experiences; makes reasonable predictions, explanations, and generalizations based on experience.	✓	✓	✓	✓		✓
Uses language to communicate findings—Develops increased vocabulary and ability to communicate observations and ideas.	✓	✓				
Collaborates—Shares materials, tasks, and ideas; collaborates in joint investigations.						

CONNECTIONS BETWEEN INQUIRY SKILLS AND OUTCOMES IN OTHER DOMAINS (CONT'D)

SOCIAL and SCIENCE	Demonstrates increasing capacity to follow rules and routines; uses materials purposefully, safely, and respectfully.	Increases abilities to compromise in interactions, take turns, and sustain interactions with peers by helping, sharing, and discussing.	Progresses in understanding similarities and respecting differences among people (such as gender, race, special needs, culture, and so on).	Develops growing awareness of jobs and what is required to perform them.
Explores/questions—Engages in open-ended explorations; forms questions that guide actions.	✓	✓	✓	✓
Begins to investigate—Engages in simple investigations to extend observations, test predictions, and pursue questions.	✓	✓	✓	✓
Collects data—Uses senses, varied tools, and simple measures to gather data.	✓	✓	✓	✓
Records and represents experience—Describes and records experiences and information through a variety of means, including two- and three-dimensional representation, charts, and movement.	✓	✓	✓	✓
Synthesizes and analyzes data from experiences—Sees patterns in data and relationships among experiences; makes reasonable predictions, explanations, and generalizations based on experience.	✓	✓	✓	✓
Uses language to communicate findings—Develops increased vocabulary and ability to communicate observations and ideas.	✓	✓	✓	✓
Collaborates—Shares materials, tasks, and ideas; collaborates in joint investigations.	✓	✓	✓	✓

APPROACHES TO LEARNING *and* SCIENCE	Chooses to participate in an increasing variety of tasks and activities, developing the ability to make independent choices.	Approaches tasks and activities with increased flexibility, imagination, and inventiveness.	Grows in eagerness to learn about and discuss a growing range of topics, ideas, and tasks.	Grows in abilities to set goals and persist in and complete a variety of tasks, activities, and projects, despite distractions or interruptions.	Develops increasing ability to find more than one solution to a question, task, or problem.	Grows in recognizing and solving problems through active exploration, interactions, and discussions with peers and adults.
Explores/questions—Engages in open-ended explorations; forms questions that guide actions.	✓	✓	✓	✓		✓
Begins to investigate—Engages in simple investigations to extend observations, test predictions, and pursue questions.	✓	✓	✓	✓	✓	✓
Collects data—Uses senses, varied tools, and simple measures to gather data.		✓	✓		✓	✓
Records and represents experience—Describes and records experiences and information through a variety of means, including two- and three-dimensional representation, charts, and movement.	✓	✓	✓	✓	✓	
Synthesizes and analyzes data from experiences—Sees patterns in data and relationships among experiences; makes reasonable predictions, explanations, and generalizations based on experience.			✓	✓	✓	✓
Uses language to communicate findings—Develops increased vocabulary and ability to communicate observations and ideas.			✓	✓		✓
Collaborates—Shares materials, tasks, and ideas; collaborates in joint investigations.		✓			✓	✓

index

Other Resources from Redleaf Press

DISCOVERING NATURE WITH YOUNG CHILDREN
by Ingrid Chalufour and Karen Worth
Education Development Center, Inc.

The first unit in the innovative Young Scientist series, *Discovering Nature with Young Children* guides teachers through an inquiry-based curriculum that builds on children's natural curiosity about the living world around them.

BUILDING STRUCTURES WITH YOUNG CHILDREN
by Ingrid Chalufour and Karen Worth
Education Development Center, Inc.

The second topic in the Young Scientist Series, *Building Structures with Young Children* guides children's explorations to help deepen their understanding of the physical science present in building block structures—including concepts such as gravity, stability, and balance.

HOLLYHOCKS AND HONEYBEES: GARDEN PROJECTS FOR YOUNG CHILDREN
by Sara Starbuck, Marla Olthof, and Karen Midden

This practical guide introduces teachers—with or without green thumbs—to the rich learning opportunities found in gardening with children.

MORE THAN MAGNETS: EXPLORING THE WONDERS OF SCIENCE IN PRESCHOOL AND KINDERGARTEN
by Sally Moomaw and Brenda Hieronymus

More Than Magnets takes the uncertainty out of teaching science. More than 100 activities engage children in interactive science opportunities—including life science, physics, and chemistry activities.

THE ART OF AWARENESS: HOW OBSERVATION CAN TRANSFORM YOUR TEACHING
by Deb Curtis and Margie Carter

Do more than watch children—*be* with children. Covering different aspects of children's lives and how to observe them, as well as giving tips for gathering and preparing documentation, *The Art of Awareness* is an inspiring look at how to see the children in your care—and how to see what they see.

MY BIG WORLD OF WONDER: ACTIVITIES FOR LEARNING ABOUT NATURE AND USING NATURAL RESOURCES WISELY
by Sherri Griffin

This easy-to-use activity book explores how we use (and ways to preserve) all natural resources: air, water, minerals, soil, land, and all life forms.

LESSONS FROM TURTLE ISLAND: NATIVE CURRICULUM IN EARLY CHILDHOOD CLASSROOMS
by Guy W. Jones and Sally Moomaw

The first complete guide to exploring Native American issues with children. Includes five cross-cultural themes—Children, Home, Families, Community, and the Environment.

800-423-8309
www.redleafpress.org